The Photographer's Guide to
Setting Up a Website

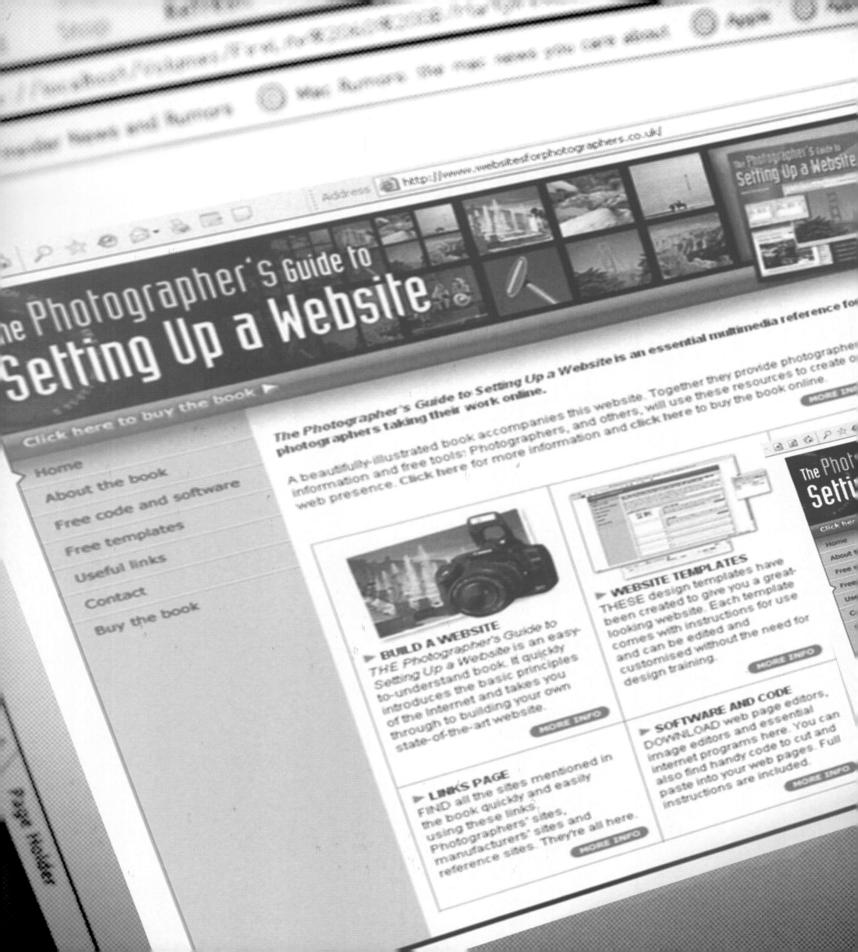

The Photographer's Guide to Setting Up a Website

MARTYN MOORE

David and Charles

A DAVID & CHARLES BOOK

David & Charles is a subsidiary of F+W (UK) Ltd.,
an F+W Publications Inc. company

First published in the UK in 2005
Reprinted 2007

Copyright © Martyn Moore 2005

Distributed in North America
by F+W Publications, Inc.
4700 East Galbraith Road
Cincinnati, OH 45236
1-800-289-0963

A catalogue record for this book is available from the British Library.

ISBN 0 7153 2092 0

Printed in Singapore by KHL Printing Co Pte Ltd
for David & Charles
Brunel House   Newton Abbot   Devon

Commissioning Editor   Neil Baber
Desk Editor   Ame Verso
Project Editor   Nicola Hodgson
Art Editor   Prudence Rogers
Designer   Louise Prentice
Production Controller   Kelly Smith

Visit our website at www.davidandcharles.co.uk

David & Charles books are available from all good bookshops; alternatively you
can contact our Orderline on (0)1626 334555 or write to us at FREEPOST EX2 110,
David & Charles Direct, Newton Abbot, TQ12 4ZZ (no stamp required UK mainland).

Contents

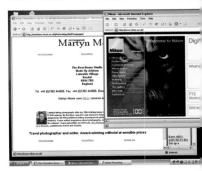

Introduction

■ **Welcome to *The Photographer's Guide to Setting Up a Website*. This book is the one that will help you to make the right decisions as you expand your photographic activity online.**

The friendly style and common-sense approach of this book makes it an ideal accompaniment to the many technical publications that are available on the subject.

Let us quickly establish a couple of things that this book is not before turning to what it is. It is not a step-by-step instruction manual on how to build a website.

The Internet uses technology that is still in its infancy and that evolves very rapidly. In the time that it takes for a book like this to go from being a manuscript to becoming a bound volume in your hands, the latest and best technology is likely to have changed and been updated several times.

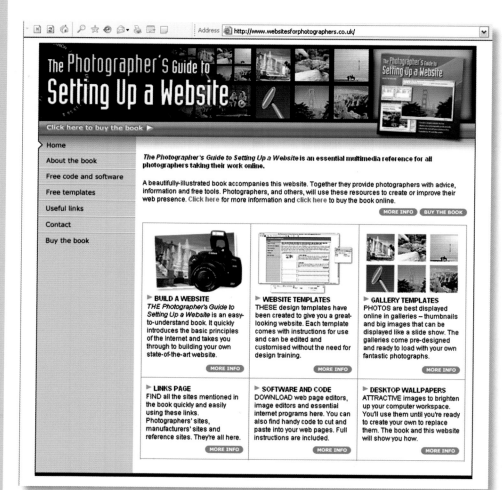

The website at www. websitesforphotographers. co.uk has been designed to accompany this book. There you will find even more examples of all the ideas and suggestions in the book, plus regular updates. You can also join in debate on the forum, and contact the team behind the book.

There are many books available on website creation from publishers who specialize in manuals that are crammed with HTML code, JavaScripts and active server page structures. Reading this book will help you to understand what these things are, but if you want to use the technology yourself, you will need to learn from a separate and complementary source.

This book is not a guarantee of business success online, but it will guide you to making the best decisions for you and give you information that will give your online presence the best possible chance of success. However, the Internet is very large and very noisy. You will need to shout very loud if you want to get yourself heard above the din.

So, if this book is not a geek's guide to web code, nor an entrepreneur's way to making a fast million, what exactly is it? Well, first of all, the aim of this guide is to help you to understand how the Internet works. It is designed to teach you what the web can do for you as a photographer and includes lots of useful advice to help you harness the power of the Internet.

This book is about making the right decisions and choices; understanding what you want from your website and what you need from it. The difference between needs and wants can be costly and time-consuming. This book assumes that you don't want your website to take over your life. It starts by taking you through the process of creating a low-cost, low-maintenance web presence. As your online profile grows, you may need to decide how best to manage your web strategy. This book will help you with that, too.

Eventually, you might have to decide between becoming a web developer in your own right, or farming out the web work to a third party and sticking with your core business. This book will help you to make that choice and, in either case, advise you on the next step.

As its name implies, the book deals primarily with the needs of photographers, but much of the information is relevant to any business that might be eyeing the web with a mixture of excitement, confusion and fear. Steven Booth has joined me in working on this project, and together we have created a website that

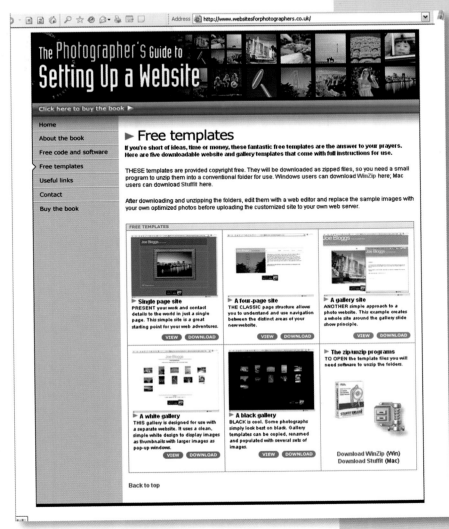

At the website you can find a selection of ready-made layout templates for you to download.

is designed to be enjoyed in conjunction with the book. The book contains many references to www. websitesforphotographers.co.uk, so use the book and the website together to see inspiring examples of ideas, follow useful links, download gallery templates and join the online community of fellow readers.

I wish you lots of enjoyment from this book and success from your adventures online.

Martyn Moore

1: Why you need your own website

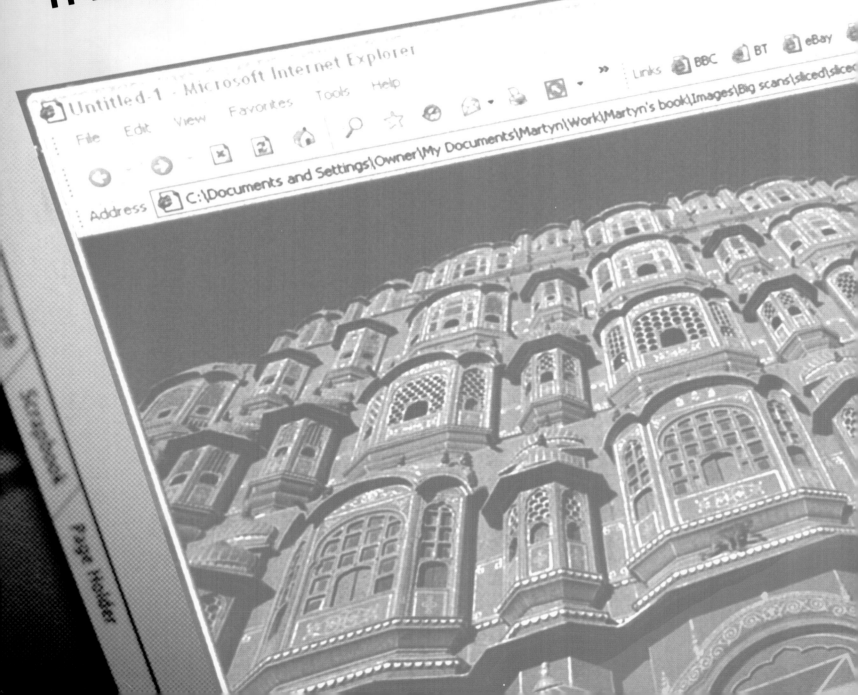

Why you need your own website

When the Internet first started to gain
in popularity, many photographers
regarded it with great suspicion. This
upstart medium seemed to be a threat
to our livelihoods. There's no doubt that
image theft occurs, but there are many
ways in which you can protect your
photographs. Overcome this obstacle,
and you will realize that the Internet offers
an unparalleled opportunity for you to
publicize your work and get your portfolio
seen by a potentially huge audience.
Creating your own website can even
lead to a full-blown business.

1 The risks and benefits

■ **Many photographers regard the Internet as a potential threat to their business. There are some issues to be aware of when it comes to protecting your images from theft and copyright infringements. However, there are simple measures that you can take to protect your work, and to enable you to use the full potential of the Internet as a marketing tool.**

The Internet: friend or foe?

For a long time, photographers were fearful of the Internet. This extraordinary new medium threatened to undermine their very existence. Any image posted on a website was sure to be duplicated innumerable times and used on other websites without credit or payment to the originator. Photographs would be stolen and printed as bootleg posters, while images downloaded, manipulated, edited and sampled would compromise the artists in much the same way that music sampling affected the record industry in the 1980s.

Many of these things happened, but the risk to photographers was far outweighed by the potential benefits. Today, many photographers understand how to manage the distribution of their images across the Internet and embrace the publicity, marketing and sales opportunities that the web can offer.

The evolution of the worldwide web

Many people still struggle to grasp the concept of the Internet, but it basically consists of millions of computers all over the world that are connected to each other to form a massive network. These computers talk to each other all the time as data, such as email, is passed between them. The Internet is a system that allows lots of people using computers to look at pages of text and pictures that are stored on lots of other computers. The pages are grouped together to form websites, each with their own address, which is often known as a 'domain' name or URL (uniform resource locator).

The Internet was first created by scientists and academics back in the 1960s. The magic really started when all these sites and pages started to link to other sites and pages. The exploration of these pages soon became a thrilling voyage of discovery.

Home computing arrived in the 1980s, along with connections to the big network via telephone wires. By the turn of the millennium, Internet shopping and surfing the web were activities as common for most people as commuting to work or going out for a drink.

The Internet and photographers

It was the Internet's ability to deliver data, files of text and images, to innumerable recipients without any clear restrictions, regulation or censorship that started to make photographers worried.

The web offered the possibility of displaying images all over the world using a digital medium that was perfect for downloading, copying and republishing images.

The extraordinary thing about digital files was that there was no loss of quality. As photographers, we knew all about copying using negatives and enlargers and contact sheets; second- and third-generation images always suffered from a slight reduction in image quality. Every copy of a digital image that is taken from a website, however, is identical to the original version. And it couldn't be easier to copy a photograph from a website onto your own personal computer. In some cases, all you need to do is drag the image from the web page onto your computer desktop.

All this made photographers rather panicky. They would insist on 'no web use' agreements and started fretting about what happened to the digital images that result when a photo is scanned for printing. Then we heard about crazy, treacherous photographers who were prepared to allow their work onto the web, sell all rights to images and see them distributed online, free of charge to anybody who wanted a copy. This seemed like madness! Some photographers tried to ignore what was happening in the hope that it would all go away.

But, of course, it hasn't gone away. The Internet, and the web of interlinked pages that span it, are here to stay. The Internet is a force to be reckoned with and then exploited to your own advantage. The risks of copyright abuse can be minimized, and, by encouraging some of the behaviours we once feared, there are some great benefits to be gained.

In fact, the risk of image theft was never that great anyway. Most images on a website are created at a low resolution of just 72 dots per inch (dpi) – that's a very coarse picture, only good for screen use. Web pictures tend to be used at quite a small size, too. If you copy an image from a website and try to print it on good-quality paper, bigger than its original size, it tends to look a mess.

Website builders are still stealing images from other people's sites, but the very fact that they do this suggests that they are not credible as businesses. Honourable web design companies with respectable clients will not steal your photographs; they would rather pay you handsomely for good work. The image pirates operate in a seedy backlot of the media; the best way to handle

them is to make their lives as difficult as possible, then ignore them.

As for those geeky guys working at computers in their bedrooms – you'd never get any money out of them for the photo they've stolen for their desktop wallpaper, so don't even think about it. Think instead about how to make it look as good as possible for them and make sure the image carries your website address discreetly in the corner. We will look at giving away free pictures as part of a marketing strategy later (see pages 120–121).

Providing free images on your website and encouraging visitors to download them is one way of protecting yourself from the picture pirates. But there are other methods, too.

These images of St Petersburg were both taken from the same original slide. The top version has 300 dots per inch (dpi) and produces an A4-sized print. The bottom version has been optimized for use on the web. The resolution is just 72dpi and uses medium JPEG compression. A print made from the bottom image would be very poor quality.

Protecting your images: copyright law

Photographers must be aware of their rights when it comes to ownership and use of their artwork. In Britain, their rights are protected under the Copyright, Designs and Patents Act 1988. This can be read or ordered online at www.opsi.gov.uk. Type the name of the document in the search box to find all references to it.

There is no such thing as worldwide international copyright, although the World Intellectual Property Organization at www.wipo.int is dedicated to establishing international conventions. In the United States, copyright information can be found at www.copyright.gov. In Europe, the European Copyright User Platform provides a wealth of information at www.eblida.org/ecup.

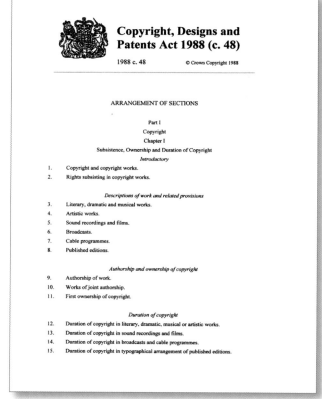

British copyright act from Her Majesty's Stationery Office.

The British copyright law clearly states that you own all rights to the images you create until you sign something that says otherwise. For example, you might enter into an agreement with a publisher to allow your picture to be printed in a book or a magazine. Unless the agreement clearly states otherwise, you still hold the copyright to that image and have granted the publisher a right to use it.

Some people mistakenly believed that the ownership of an image was somehow associated with ownership and development of the film it was taken on. That theory was finally discarded with the advent of digital cameras, but it never really stood up anyway. The law states that even staff photographers hold the rights to the images that they create for their employers, although most bosses these days issue contracts that cover copyright. Once signed, these turn the rights to the photographer's work over to the company.

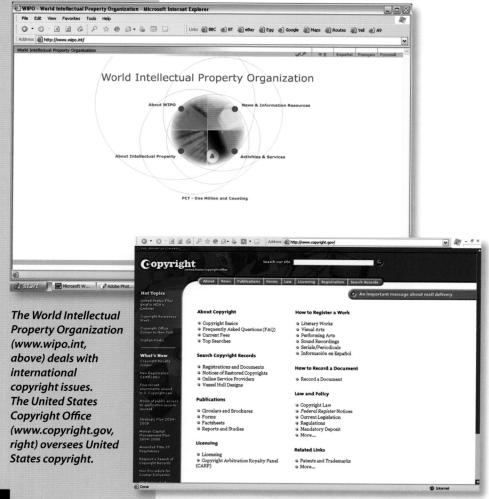

The World Intellectual Property Organization (www.wipo.int, above) deals with international copyright issues. The United States Copyright Office (www.copyright.gov, right) oversees United States copyright.

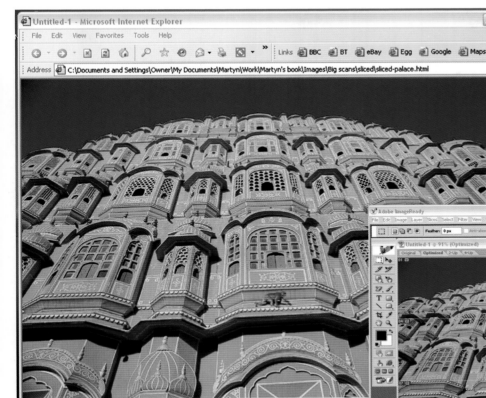

Adobe's ImageReady slices up images and writes the HTML code to put them together again in a web page (below). You can see the individual slices opened in Photoshop (bottom). The image is reassembled in a web page (left). Slicing an image helps to deter copying.

Protecting your images: practical methods

There are also several practical methods of protecting your work on the Internet. First of all, only use pictures with a low resolution. Computer screens show 72dpi, so putting images with 150dpi on your website is a waste of time unless you actually want people to download them and make prints. Don't display images on your site any bigger than you have to – the bigger the picture, the more attractive it is to the browser burglar.

Your photo-editing software offers security measures, too. One simple deterrent is to cut an image up into two, three or more slices and then put them back together in the design of the page. Anybody trying to download a photograph discovers they have to download three images and then put them back together. If they are determined, this method won't stop them, but if they're lazy, it might persuade them to look for an easier option elsewhere.

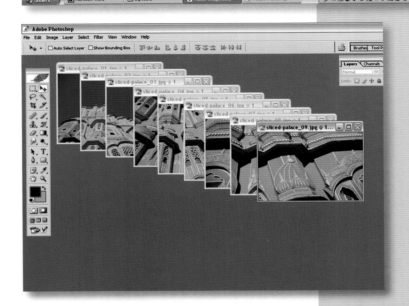

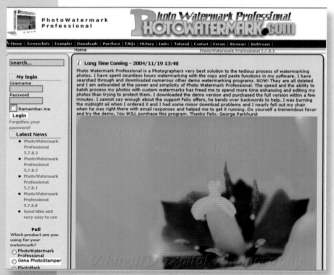

Lots of photo-editing packages allow you to 'watermark' your images. This can take the form of a message or shape that looks as if it has been stamped, or embossed, into the image. The distortion that is created is not enough to destroy the quality of the image, and the subject matter remains clear, but the picture can't be used elsewhere without your branding remaining on it for all to see. You can stamp images with your name, your logo or your web address.

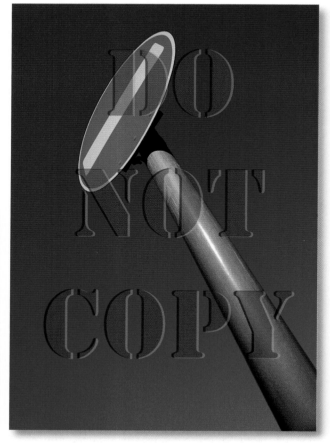

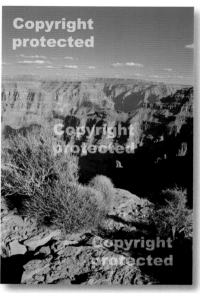

Each of these images has been given a 'watermark' that allows the photograph to be appreciated but that prevents its use on other websites.

The code to generate this pop-up message is available from the website at www.websitesforphotographers.co.uk. If a visitor to this page tries to copy the image by clicking the right-hand mouse button, their browser will flash up this message. The wording of the message can be edited, so the feature can also be used to promote sales of an image or to provide contact information.

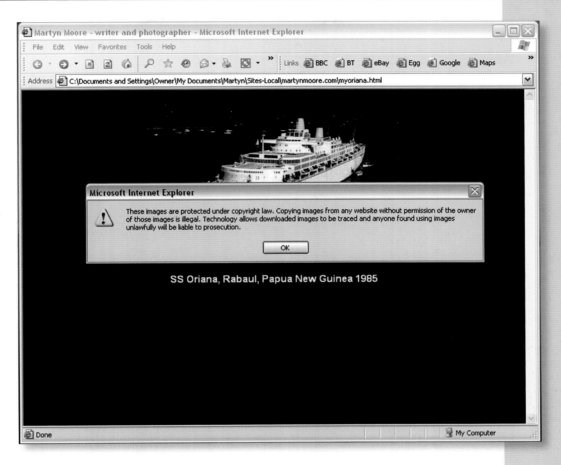

Another method that you can use to protect your images is to include bits of code or scripts when images are designed into your web page that make copying by right-clicking or dragging with the mouse difficult. Any attempt at copying an image in this way will result in the user's computer 'pinging' at them and a warning message appearing on the screen.

At this stage, it is worth mentioning the sort of tone that you adopt when writing warnings about copyright infringement. Whether you use a message in the watermark technique, have a pop-up warning message or a simple statement somewhere on your website, the message should be short, simple and clear. Do not rant or make abusive threats that you are unlikely to carry out if the offender is twice your size. An effective form of wording might be: 'These images are protected under copyright law. Copying images from any website without permission of the owner of those images is illegal.

Technology allows downloaded images to be traced and anyone found using images unlawfully will be liable to prosecution.'

Sometimes, a touch of humour might be equally effective: 'Please don't steal my images. Ring +44 7768 261276 and offer me money to create some better photographs just for you.'

You can see examples of all these methods on the website that accompanies this book, at www.websitesforphotographers.co.uk.

Ultimately, you will still get picture pirates attempting to steal your images, and the most tenacious will succeed. But if you are an innovative and creative photographer, with a prolific output of new material, you have to ask yourself, 'so what?' Serious clients with good money looking for original work are the people you really want to catch, so keep your mind and energies directed towards attracting them.

A business strategy

■ **The Internet presents an unparalleled marketing method to businesses in general and photographers in particular. This is your opportunity to show your work to the largest potential audience in the world. Businesses are now so aware of the importance of the Internet to their success that it is very rare to find one without some sort of web presence. If you want to be a success, you need a website, too.**

The best marketing tool

The web has been described as the single most powerful marketing tool ever. Considering the impact that television has had on our lives, that might seem like a grand statement. But the major difference with the Internet is the low cost and speed with which you can put content on it. Within minutes, you can create a simple, virtually free web page that shows a sample of your work and carries all your contact details – even a direct email link. That page can be viewed within seconds by anyone with a computer connected to the Internet, anywhere in the world. All they have to do is find it.

The idea is quite extraordinary. People in Australia, America, China and Wales can see your web page as easily as people in the next town. Admittedly, Australia might not be your target market, and people in Wales might not be interested in your web page, but the concept is still impressive.

The Internet works just as effectively at the extremes of its reach. At the global end, there's nothing quite like it. It brings together people with specific interests all around the world like nothing has ever done before. Stamp collectors in Stamford can email philatelists in Philadelphia while looking at the same websites. More stamps move around. At the local level, people living in the same street can organize barbecues and the weekend sporting activities around a community website and electronic newsletter. More socializing is done.

The Internet has transformed businesses that are built around a specialist interest. This stamp dealer can serve a global market far more easily than ever before.

This restaurant website is hosted on free webspace and provides a huge amount of information: menu; opening hours; delivery information; contact details and even fun quotes from the staff.

Businesses on the web

People now usually expect a modern business to have a website. This has become an accepted part of modern culture, particularly now Internet shopping is more and more commonplace. Can you think of any successful brand that isn't on the web in some way? Directory sites operate at local and global levels and publish details of businesses via searchable databases, so even companies without a website are likely to be listed on somebody else's site. People even look up the telephone number of a restaurant on the Internet when they want to order take-away food.

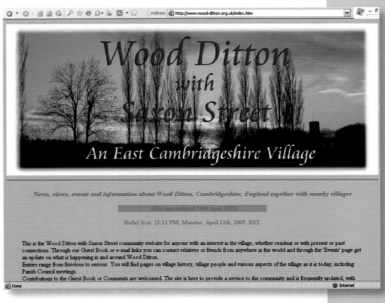

Local groups can pursue their own agenda online. Although these sites can be seen anywhere in the world, their content is aimed at visitors within a short distance of the region.

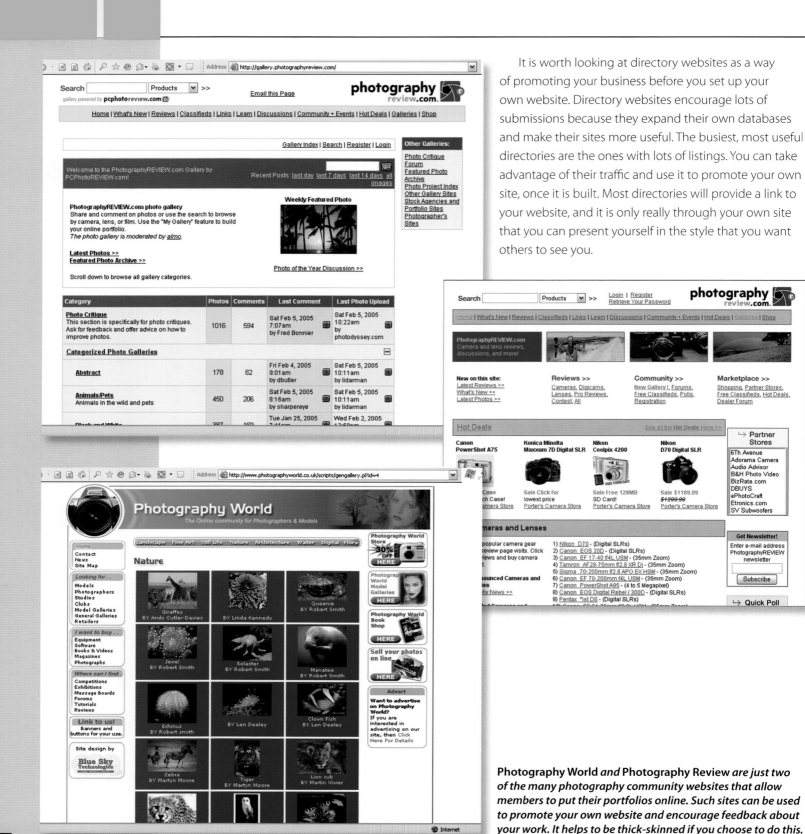

It is worth looking at directory websites as a way of promoting your business before you set up your own website. Directory websites encourage lots of submissions because they expand their own databases and make their sites more useful. The busiest, most useful directories are the ones with lots of listings. You can take advantage of their traffic and use it to promote your own site, once it is built. Most directories will provide a link to your website, and it is only really through your own site that you can present yourself in the style that you want others to see you.

Photography World *and* **Photography Review** *are just two of the many photography community websites that allow members to put their portfolios online. Such sites can be used to promote your own website and encourage feedback about your work. It helps to be thick-skinned if you choose to do this.*

Images posted on review websites usually appear in a gallery and reveal a bigger version when clicked. There is room to add technical and location details, and you can create your own profile to be viewed when visitors click on your name.

Your portfolio on the web

Even if you can't yet see the advantage to your business of having an Internet presence, surely you would like people to see your work. The thrill of an exhibition or publication is something that many photographers like to think about. It is wonderful to be able to share your pictures with a wider audience, and nothing presents you to a wider audience than the Internet. If you are really brave, you might even encourage people to tell you what they think of your work.

Websites can be great levellers. You might be just one photographer with a Nikon, three lenses and a bagful of film, but if your pictures are good there is no reason why your website shouldn't be as impressive as any world-famous photographer's. This is not about subterfuge; it's about presenting yourself in a way that doesn't result in clients judging you by the age of your car and the state of the carpet in your office, but by what really counts: the quality of your photographic work. Get your website right, get a few good jobs under your belt, and the new car and soft carpet will follow.

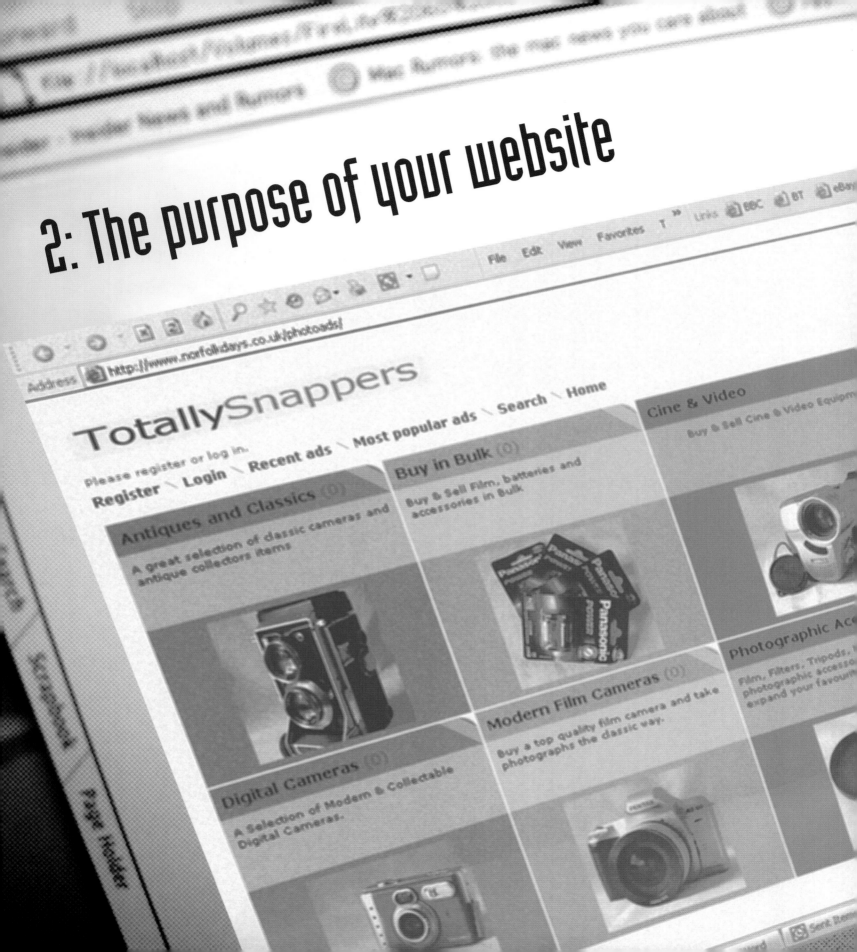

2: The purpose of your website

2:

The purpose of your website

There's no doubt that having your own website can be a tremendous advantage to you as a photographer. However, before you start thinking about the design and content of your site, you need to be absolutely clear about what you want your site to do for you. It can simply be a means of getting your work seen by the public. On the other hand, it can be your principal means of winning commissions and earning an income. Once you have decided what your website should do, you can think about its design and content.

2 | Clarifying your aims

You need to have a clear idea of what you want your website to do for you. Do you simply want to display your work in a public arena? Do you want to increase awareness and generate commissions? Do you want to sell photographs and prints? Would you like to receive feedback from your audience? You need to decide at the outset what features are important to you so that these facilities can be designed into your website.

Purpose dictates design

Like television, radio and print, the Internet is a medium for the exchange of information. It can carry advertising and editorial and it can sell directly. What a website is required to do dictates virtually all aspects of its design.

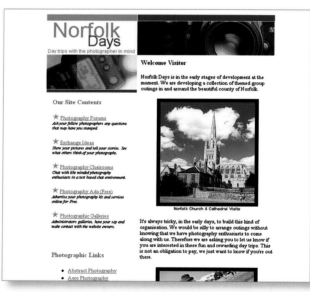

Norfolk Days aims to inform and inspire photographers in the region. Advice, inspiration and technique dominate.

Some websites are packed with information and, hopefully, visitors will find them useful places to be. Other sites provide entertainment or a pleasant environment that visitors can enjoy; they can come away enlightened but not necessarily better informed. And, of course, websites can provide a combination of the two.

Where the emphasis is placed will dictate which features on a site are essential, which are desirable, and which would be a luxury or indulgence but could be omitted if time or money gets tight.

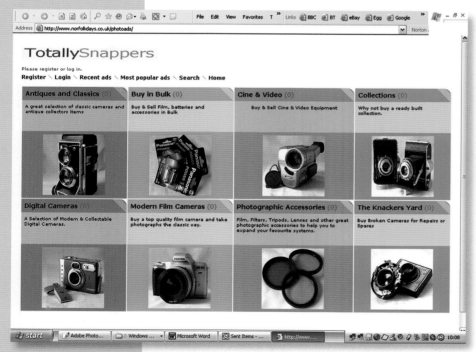

This site is built around buying and selling camera equipment, so product pictures and descriptions lead the design.

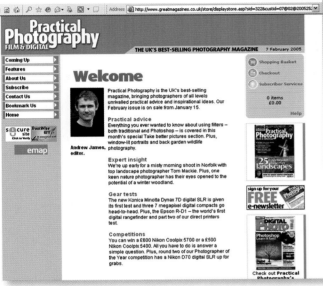

The publishers of **Practical Photography** *magazine decided that the main purposes of its website (below) was to sell magazines, subscriptions and collect registration data for a regular e-newsletter.*

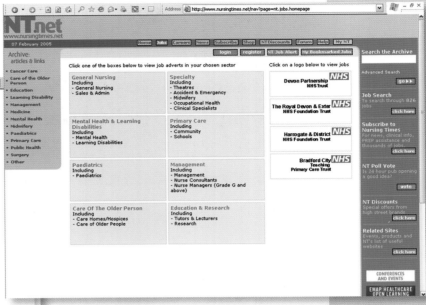

The company behind **Practical Photography** *also publishes* **Nursing Times** *and dedicates much of its online effort (above) to recruitment advertising.*

If a site is to be information-laden, then it might be best sitting on a database with some kind of search facility provided on the page to help users find what they want. If you want people to communicate with you via your website, then one or more of the many Internet dialogue options, such as email links, message boards and chat, can be built in.

An example from the real world

In the previous section, we looked at the advantages to businesses of having websites. It is easy merely to say, 'Well, we have to have a website. We just do. Everybody else has one.' That belief might be motivation enough. However, in 2000 a major magazine publishing company challenged the prevailing view and saved itself a lot of time and money by deciding that it would not start setting up websites just then.

The reason why that company decided to delay web development was because it looked further than the 'We have to have websites' belief, to ask the question, 'What do we want our websites to do?' The magazine brands

all answered: 'Everything!' Given that some of the things that websites do can be expensive to create, clearly 'everything' was going to cost a fortune.

Managers and marketers were told to narrow the brief down considerably; they needed come up with a single, simple objective that would define a website's purpose. They were sent back to their desks and their creative teams to have a proper think.

Years later, many of those brands have excellent websites, each with a very clear purpose. Some still don't have sites, while others have devised brilliant ways of using the web as a communication and sales tool without having a permanent web presence. They regularly send out engaging HTML emails, designed like websites, to subscribers' email addresses (see page 113).

Those publishers were initially seduced by the speed and variety offered by the technology. The multimedia, interactive, real-time potential was attractive to people who had been using just paper and ink for years. But by pausing to consider exactly what a website could achieve for a brand, these publishers have been able to exploit the full potential of having a web presence.

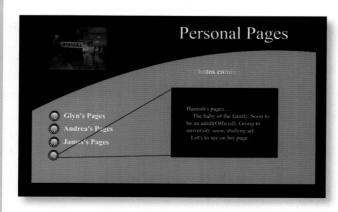

Simple display websites

You need to be clear at an early stage about what you want your website to achieve. Maybe you just want to display your photography to a wider audience. That's fine. Showing off is a natural and satisfying thing to do. It's good to be proud of your work, and impressing those you can share it with feels great.

If displaying your work is your primary purpose, do you want to show the world what a great photographer you are, or do you want people to be impressed by your great website? The impressive-photographer approach is easy for us to handle right here in this book; the fancy-website approach might require you to look beyond these pages and, unless you have plenty of money, you might need to consider a career change. That's fine – many talented photographers have gone on to become great web designers, too.

Let's assume, however, that you don't want to become a web designer just yet; your primary purpose is to launch your photographic talent on an unsuspecting world.

If you are just interested in displaying your images, you might not be that concerned about generating more work. Perhaps you have another job and photography is just a hobby. In that case, your website could be the online equivalent of presenting your holiday slideshow to a silent (but hopefully appreciative) audience. 'There you go!' you're saying. 'This is me and my work. Take it or leave it.' And they will.

This is the quickest and easiest kind of website to build and, if you read quickly enough, you could even have one online in a few hours from now. Your work will be online, you can tell people your web address, you'll have got the whole thing off your chest and you can leave it at that.

But you know it won't end there, of course. You can update the site with new masterpieces any time you like and use it to complement the annual family newsletter at Christmas. Include the web address to make sure that your cousins in Australia can share your holiday snaps and the pictures of the new house extension.

Websites with feedback facilities

Many of you will want your websites to go further than being simple display sites. The next stage is to create an online exhibition where feedback and critique are important. Some of us want to know what people think of our work and, although it might smart somewhat at the time, can happily take criticism in the belief that it can be used to make us better photographers.

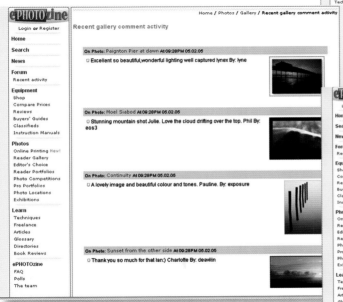

Some critique from ePHOTOzine *users.*

The simplest type of feedback mechanism you can provide is an email link. When a user clicks this link on your web page, the email program on their computer opens and a new message is created with your email address already in the 'To:' field. Text can automatically be added to the 'Subject:' field of the message, too; this can be made to say something like: 'I've visited your website and here's what I think of your photographs.'

Photography community websites already exist that welcome photographic submissions from people seeking feedback. Interested visitors can browse online portfolios and post their comments for all to see. The critique can be kind or cruel, and the most controversial opinions often

generate a flurry of responses from others who may side with the photographer or the critic.

Some of these sites are huge and, although they attract many visitors, the volume of other photographers' submissions might dilute the impact of an individual's work. This type of critique can be added to your own site by providing a message or bulletin board facility and including it on pages with photographs that you would like to receive comments on. Providing this feature on your site is not a good idea if you have a fragile ego. You will be allowing people to critique your work in public.

Visitors to ePHOTOzine *are encouraged to comment on camera equipment and to join the many photography-related debates, such as digital versus traditional and the ethics of image retouching.*

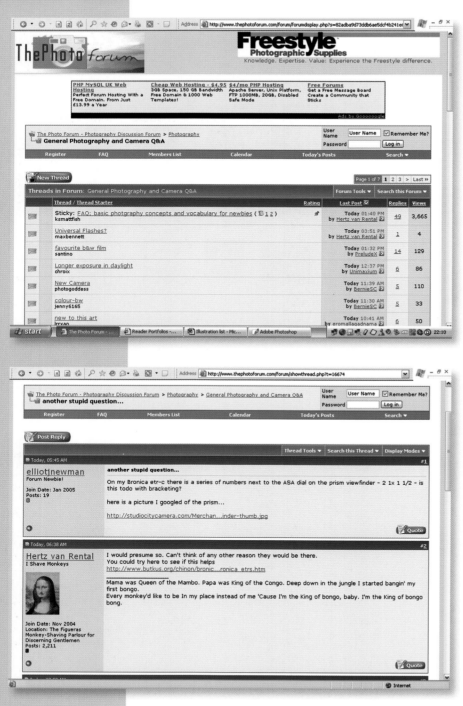

Discussion boards and forum activity on a dedicated forum site. Regulars on a site like this dispense accurate and useful advice and information. Many don't use their real names, though. Always keep on the lookout for the rogues who disrupt the discussions.

Providing this facility also takes you to the first level of ongoing maintenance. At the very least, you will look at the site to see what comments people are making. You might receive unwelcome feedback that you want to remove from the page, and there will be an enormous temptation to dive onto the site and post your own defence of your pictures. One word of advice here: don't. Remove the offensive postings, by all means, but arguing with a critic on your own website after inviting feedback will not place you in a favourable light.

Lots of online services can offer you a message-board feature for a small monthly fee. There are free options, too, which involve displaying other people's advertising on your pages. You can also create a series of boards of your own if you have the right technical facilities and buy or license the software.

By offering increased levels of interaction on your website, you start to create a sense of community. People will begin to interact with each other and discussions that start off around you and your work can go off at all sort of unexpected tangents.

Websites for professional promotion

The next considerations are for those of you who want to create a website to promote yourself professionally. Everything so far in this chapter can be applied equally by both amateurs and professionals. Professionals need to carefully consider the time it will take to maintain their websites. They might not care so much about what people think of their work, beyond the question: 'Are you going to use me, or not?'

The simplest website for you if you are a professional photographer will describe what you do, show one or two examples of your work, and give clear and detailed information about how you can be contacted. This can all be achieved on one single web page.

The next level will involve separating these elements, and possibly adding extra information such as a biography or a list of clients, and putting them on different pages, each one linked to all the others. This is the first move from a web page to a website. It is

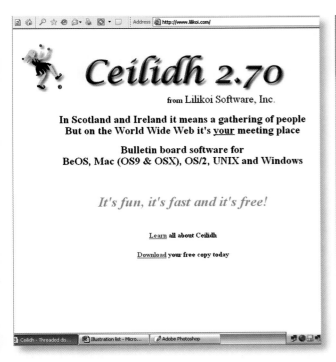

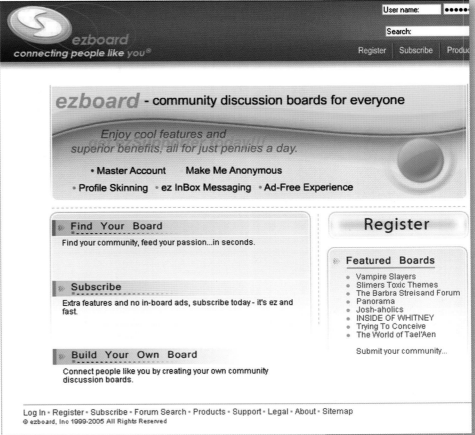

equivalent to the difference between having a business card or leaflet and a brochure or catalogue.

Pictures can also be organized into galleries – we will look at how easily you can do that later (see pages 130–131). There are some fantastic gallery templates for you to download from the website that goes with this book, www.websitesforphotographers.co.uk, for you to use on your own website.

Interaction on the site might focus around customers' enquiries, such as day rates, availability, and rights to pictures. Really sophisticated features might include an online booking facility where a customer can access a calendar feature on your site and check your availability. This can be made to synchronize with your diary or organizer software. Many things are possible.

Selling your work online

It is even possible to use your website to sell your work online. Art photography can be ordered from a website, paid for and then dispatched to the customer just like any other type of mail order. You can offer digital versions of your photographs for customers

to download for use in publications or to print out themselves for their walls.

As soon as you decide you want to conduct business directly over the Internet – money and supply transactions right from your website – you have to consider security. Although no Internet payment system can be completely secure (as no credit card-based system is infallible), many of them are now well tried and trusted. There is a section dedicated to e-commerce later in this book (see pages 122–125).

As you can see, with so many options available, so many levels of sophistication to consider, it is easy to be tempted by the possibilities. You can be forgiven for wanting everything, and trying to do it all. Stop for a minute though. Think carefully about what you want to achieve. Consider the time and money that you have to spend. Be specific, keep focus, and stay calm.

Two of the many websites offering message-board facilities for other websites. These services have ways of earning money for their providers – you might find advertisements served on your forum or messages sent to your registered users. Try to find out how the operators work before you install the service.

3: Building your website

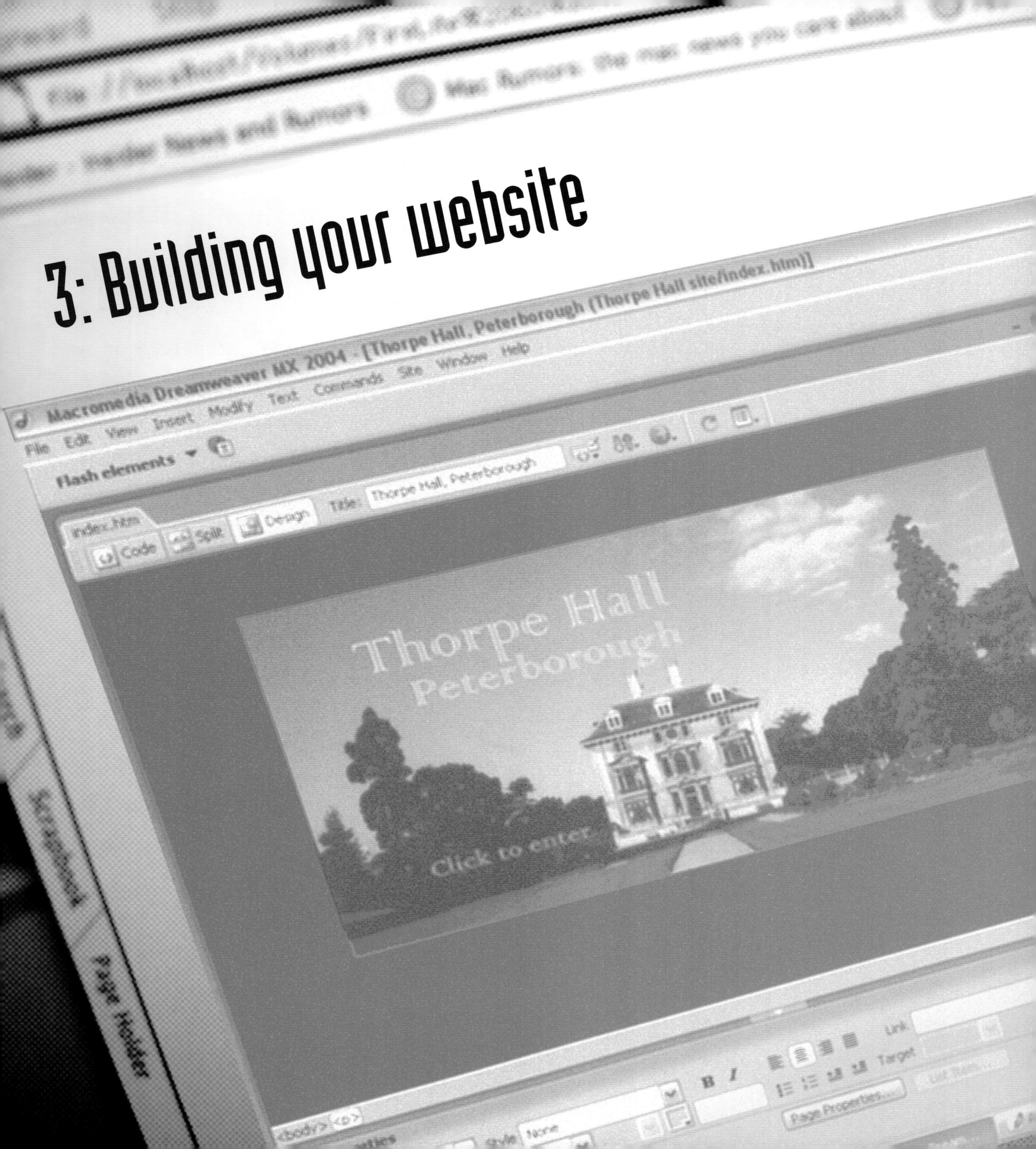

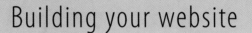

3:

Building your website

You might think that you need some very abstruse skills to be able to create your own website; in fact, it's relatively simple. There's a good chance that you already have software loaded on your computer with which to create a site. Even the more specialized software is now much more accessible and intuitive. You can pay someone to build a website for you, of course, but if you learn how to do it yourself you will save money, educate yourself and equip yourself well should you have to deal with a professional web builder in the future.

3 Why build your own website?

You can pay a professional web designer to create a site for you, but there are many advantages to learning these skills for yourself. The obvious one is that of cost; doing it yourself will save you money. In addition, being clued up on website design puts you in a stronger position should you decide to commission a professional designer in the future.

The advantages of creating your own site

You're a very busy person, and there are so many web designers springing up all over the place that there's even a section for them in the local telephone directory. So, why would you want to build your own website?

Well, there are several reasons to consider it. The main one is cost. Web designers are not cheap. They have skills that have taken time and probably money to acquire and they're in demand right now, so you're going to have to pay for them. Of course, there is the option of using a young student who wants to earn a bit of beer money. Good luck if that's the path you choose.

There are many advantages to building your own website. It will give you a basic understanding of the medium, the technology, and the potential. Armed with this knowledge, you can go on to commission a website from a professional from an informed position. You will know what you are talking about. Without that knowledge, it would be like going to buy a car before you can drive or have any idea where you will go and what you will use it for.

Print publication pages created with Adobe InDesign, like this magazine cover, can be saved as web pages.

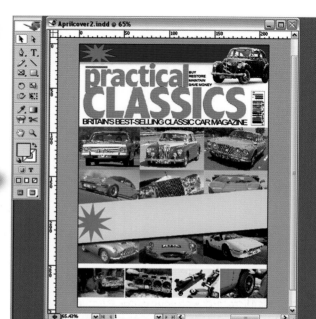

Microsoft PowerPoint is normally used for presentations using text, pictures and graphic special effects. By choosing Save As ..., a PowerPoint document can be converted into a multi-page website with many of the effects retained.

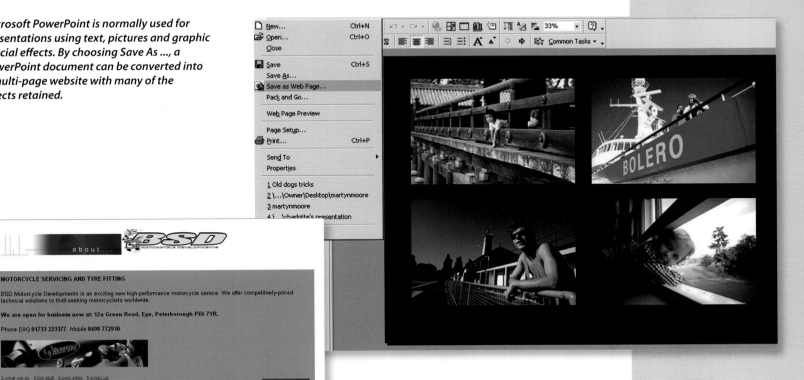

Microsoft Word documents can also be saved as HTML web pages. By choosing Save As Web Page, an HTML page is created with links to a new folder containing copies of the images that you have used.

FrontPage is Microsoft's web page editor. It has a similar look and feel to programs such as Word and PowerPoint.

Another reason for creating your own site is that it is very simple. HTML, the basic language of simple web pages, has become an almost-universal file format on computers, and lots of software packages offer the option of saving a document as a web page. Professional desktop publishing software programs such as Quark XPress and Adobe InDesign will allow pages of words and pictures to be saved as a web page.

Microsoft PowerPoint is excellent for creating screen presentations with images and effects and that, too, has a 'save as web page' option. Even Microsoft Word will convert documents with images, tables and formatted text into HTML versions. Both PowerPoint and Word are part of the Microsoft Office suite of programs and if you have Office, then you probably have FrontPage – Microsoft's own web page editor. And by following instructions in Chapter 7 (see pages 82–85), you will learn how to create a simple single web page in Microsoft Works' Word Processor – a program that is preloaded on to almost all new computers.

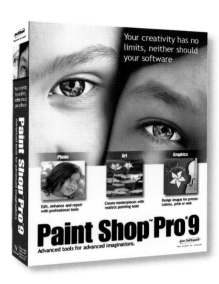

Paint Shop Pro is a powerful image editor with many of the features that are found in Photoshop but at a fraction of the price. The developer, Jasc, is now owned by Corel.

Macromedia Dreamweaver is a dedicated web page design program with powerful page and image linking applications and style sheet features. It integrates with other Macromedia products such as Flash and Fireworks.

Web design packages and image editors

At the same time that popular, easy-to-use software is becoming web-enabled, the specialized, once-complex web design packages are becoming more intuitive and user-friendly. One of the most popular web design packages is Macromedia Dreamweaver. This can be downloaded for free trial from the Macromedia website (www.macromedia.com) and easy-to-follow user guides will show you how to create a simple web page in minutes. If Dreamweaver doesn't suit you, there are many other web design applications to consider before you spend any money.

In addition to design programs, you will need a decent digital image editor. You will at least need to be able to adjust the size, resolution and compression of your images to make them suitable for the web. The resolution (or grain, to use a photography term), of web images is 72dpi and the common file format is the compressed JPEG (.jpg) file. Your image-editing program should be capable of making these from other types of image files.

The good news here is that you probably already have an adequate image-editing program. Microsoft Paint is preloaded on most PCs, but isn't quite up to the job. However, if you have a digital camera or a decent scanner

then the software supplied with these products is almost certainly powerful enough.

The best image editors include Corel Paint Shop Pro and Adobe Photoshop. Photoshop has managed to earn itself the tag of being the industry standard, but it is quite expensive. Paint Shop Pro is just as good in many ways, but is much cheaper.

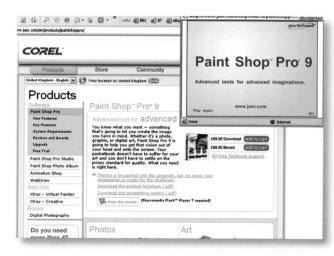

Keen digital photographers will already be using a sophisticated image-editing package. If you haven't tried one yet, most are available as trial versions.

If you are prepared to pay the price associated with the industry standard, you won't find a better image editor than Adobe Photoshop.

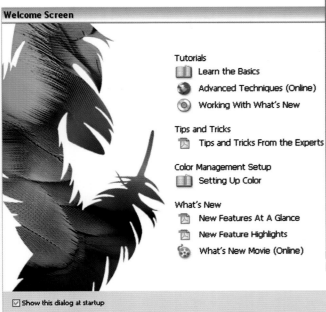

Transferring web page files

Finally, you might find you need a small program for transferring web page files from your local computer (the one on your desk) to the one that hosts your site on the Internet. The process used for this is called File Transfer Protocol (FTP). Most of the services that host websites (these are discussed in more detail in the next section; see pages 34–37) will be able to provide details on how to upload your web pages using this system.

FrontPage and Dreamweaver can upload files via FTP, but if you create a web page using a word processing package then you will need a separate FTP program. There are several that you can obtain for free; we have posted two of these on the website at www. websitesforphotographers.co.uk.

Before you part with any cash for software, see how much you can do for free. You might be surprised, and that money might be better put towards professional help at a later date.

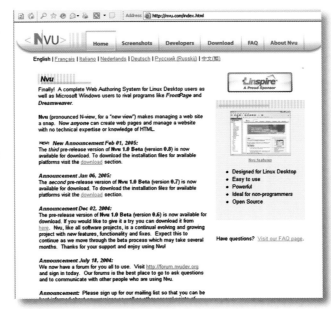

Nvu is a free web editor available for Macs and PCs with Windows or other operating systems. It follows the conventions of most other web editors, so it feels quite familiar. The program is being developed constantly; the latest version is available from www.websitesforphotographers.co.uk.

A cost-effective website

If you have access to the Internet, either at home, at work or from a public library, a business centre or an Internet café, then you could create your own free website in minutes. And with the investment of just a small amount of money, you can create a really good site that will be an asset to your business.

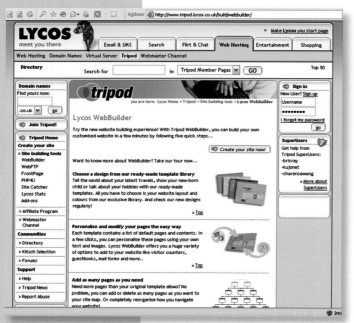

Two of the best-known free web space providers are Tripod, now owned by Lycos, and GeoCities, which is part of Yahoo!

Finding free web space

Hundreds of companies offer 'free' web space and many different ways of creating pages on that web space. Tripod (www.tripod.co.uk) is one of the longest-established companies doing this. It makes its money by putting advertisements around the pages you create.

A possible downside of the host placing adverts around your web pages is that those adverts are often generated by clever software that recognizes the content of your site. It uses keywords found in the name of your site and the text on your pages to attempt to generate

relevant adverts around your site. There is a good chance, therefore, that a photography-based site will carry photography-linked advertisements, and you might find a rival photographer's site being promoted on yours! You just need to hope that your site is better than theirs – which it will be, of course, because you're reading this book.

Internet service providers almost always offer 'free' web space to their customers, which is paid for in the cost of the subscription. Pay-as-you-surf Internet services usually only allow their customers to work on their websites via their own pay-per-minute connections so they get revenue that way. A good example of this

Lycos offers website builders a range of services. Webmonkey provides technical advice and information at all levels from web experts and professionals.

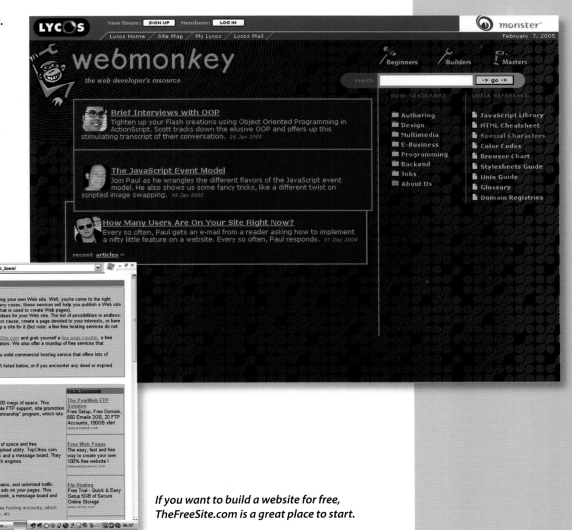

If you want to build a website for free, TheFreeSite.com is a great place to start.

type of web space is offered at www.virgin.net and the pioneering Internet provider Freeserve, which has been bought out and is now found at www.wanadoo.co.uk. This will allow you to build a website on its space whether or not you connect with Wanadoo.

Creating the website

All of these services offer websites that are built using templates viewed through your web browser. The templates are becoming increasingly stylish and sophisticated, although they tend to cater more for the personal homepage builder, often using section names

such as 'My Hobbies' and 'My Favourite Links'.

You will be offered a selection of layouts with colour co-ordinated graphics. Text-editing tools allow you to change and format the copy in panels, lists and captions and there will be instructions on how to upload pictures to the positions predetermined in the design of the pages. All you have to do is decide what you want to say and show.

This tip could save you a lot of heartache if you experience technical problems: keep copies of everything you create. Because the website-building process takes place in a semi-live environment, your text and picture creation can be lost if your computer crashes, the host's

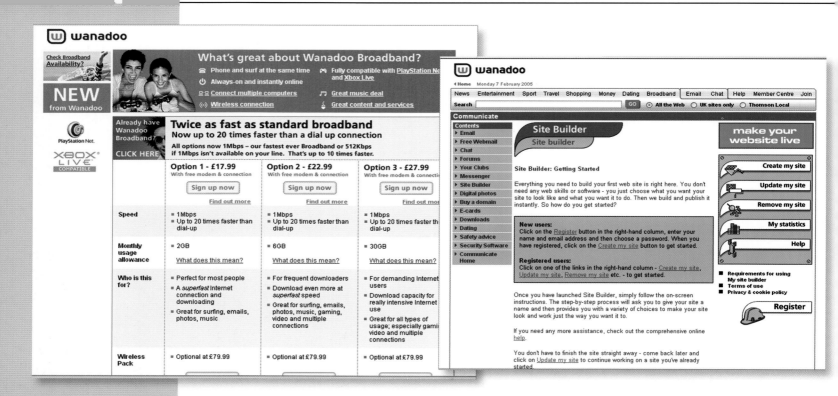

Almost every Internet service provider (ISP) offers personal web space with its connection accounts. Some allow this space to be used for business purposes. Broadband accounts are starting to be metered, with charges applied according to the amount of data transferred across your connection. Uploading files to your web space will affect this, and if your website attracts lots of traffic you might incur higher charges. Read the terms and conditions carefully.

computers crash or your connection to the Internet is broken for some reason.

One insurance policy is to gather all the text and images that you intend to publish on your website into one dedicated folder on your computer's hard drive. Rather than write the 150-word introduction online, write it in a text or Word document on your local machine, save it, and then publish it on your website using the cut-and-paste process. Similarly, you will need to create versions of your photographs with a resolution of 72dpi and cropped to suit their position on the page. Save these processed images in the same folder as the text on your own machine and call them up from this folder when you publish them on your website.

Then, if the computer crashes or the website host goes out of business, you still have all the elements that were used to create the pages. This process is also good for getting you into the right frame of mind for creating a site on your local machine and then publishing it on the web, like the professionals do. It introduces the concept of gathering all your website assets into one place, clearly

organized in an order that will save you lots of time and spare you lots of frustration. There's a whole section dedicated to this later on pages 62–65.

A more sophisticated approach

Community-based sites such as Tripod are great places to start to play. They get you into the basics and offer smart, ready-made web pages. However, there is a good chance that your pages will be almost identical to thousands of other people's pages.

You might want to take the next step and start to create your website with a unique design, or at least one with an artistic or photographic feel to it. We have created a small range of photo-style templates for you to try on our own website at www.websitesforphotographers.co.uk. There you will also find links to examples of the websites referred to in this chapter and an online step-by-step guide to downloading pages and templates, editing them on your own machine and republishing them using the FTP process. There is more on this on pages 86–87.

Investing in broadband

If you have bought this book, you have already made one small investment in your website. It's time to make another two. The first is to sign up with an Internet service provider that offers broadband service. There are two major benefits to this: first, you will publish your site much more quickly. Second, broadband suppliers tend to offer a more 'serious' web space and email package to their customers. Spending a moderate amount of money a month will get you a large amount of web space (50Mb is a BIG website) and fast, easy access to it. Every country has its own Internet service providers, often linked to national telecommunications companies. Germany's T-Online service from Deutsche Telekom is the biggest ISP in Europe; Wanadoo is reaching out from its French origins; and Tiscali is extending from its Italian base. America Online, better known as AOL, has been offering international Internet services for several years. The effect of this globalization has been to standardize services and pricing, with great benefits to the consumer, who rather than being bewildered by choice, can hardly go wrong.

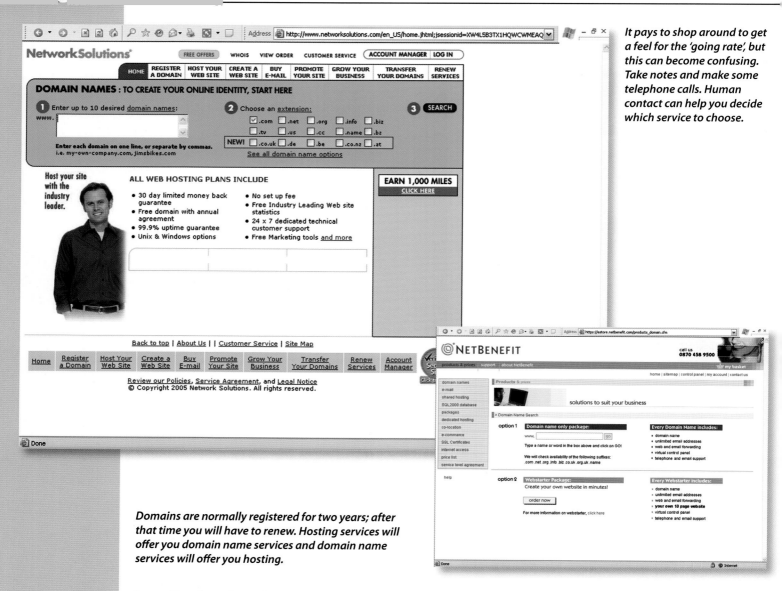

It pays to shop around to get a feel for the 'going rate', but this can become confusing. Take notes and make some telephone calls. Human contact can help you decide which service to choose.

Domains are normally registered for two years; after that time you will have to renew. Hosting services will offer you domain name services and domain name services will offer you hosting.

Investing in a domain name

The other small but vital investment is in a domain name. All the web space that we have discussed so far is accessed by an obscure website address. Look at the online examples we have created for you. All those web addresses contain the name of the hosting company, with only part of the address relevant to the site name.

You want your website to be called something like www.yourname.com or www.yourcompany.co.uk and to get that you need to register the domain name. Hundreds of Internet service providers will register a domain name for you. Prices vary, so shop around. Our own website offers the facility to search for a suitable domain name and it carries links to companies who will register that name for you. The companies we recommend offer a service called 'web forwarding' so you can still build your site on the 'free' space we have talked about in this chapter. Then, when you register and advertise your own domain name, visitors who type this in will be redirected to your free web space and the long, irrelevant web address will be hidden by your snappy personal address.

Brokers will offer you the best deal, but all domain names are registered and administered centrally. With some sites you have to 'de-select' the domain names you don't want, so there is a risk that you accidentally buy the .com, the .org, the .biz versions and others if you are not careful. Also make sure that you will be the registrant, not the broker.

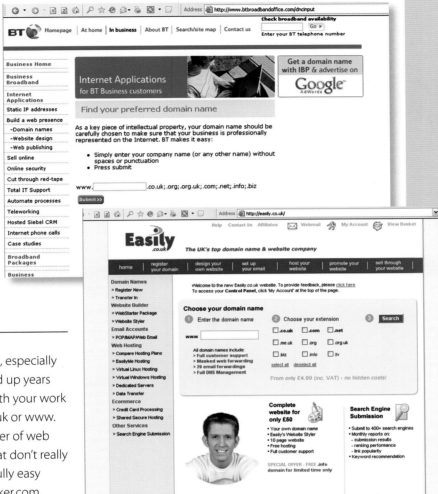

Choosing a domain name

Choosing your domain name can be stressful, especially if your name is fairly normal and was snapped up years ago by a magician. Combining your name with your work might help: www.paulwattsphotography.co.uk or www.jimspics.com. And there are a growing number of web brands that have snappy-sounding words that don't really mean anything but that are short and hopefully easy to remember: www.zapsnap.net or www.clicker.com. We thought carefully about the web address for the site that accompanies this book. We decided that www.thephotographersguidetosettingupawebsite.com was probably too long. Instead we edited it a bit and used the UK domain to be clear about where we are based. Hence www.websitesforphotographers.co.uk – shorter, descriptive and easier to remember.

Take your time thinking about how you'd like to be known online. Also remember that, although your web identity is important, you don't have to be stuck forever with the name that you choose. You can pay a small amount of money for registration costs for two years; you might have a great domain name idea weeks or months from now; or previously registered names might again become available.

It is normally quite easy to contact someone who might have already registered the name that you like. If they are not using it, they might be persuaded to sell it to you. But don't be tempted to pay over the odds for a name as this just encourages web piracy and cybersquatting. Your online identity is quite important, but don't be held to ransom for it.

Spend some time experimenting with web community sites, try different suppliers and services and get hooked up to broadband. Buy your domain name and point it at your home page. You will have a website, you will own a domain name, and you are well and truly online. You could stop now. But you won't.

4: The look of your website

4:

The look of your website

Once you are clear about exactly what you want your website to do for you and your business, you can decide what sort of look will best promote your aims. You might be drawn to an arty, innovative look, or a more straightforward, commercial design. Once you have made this broad choice, you can focus on the specifics such as choice of font and colour. This section also outlines the basic mistakes to avoid – the garish, unreadable combinations of colours, the obscure fonts and the intros that take forever to open.

What look works for you?

Just a few years ago, all websites looked the same. They consisted simply of pages of text and images; you started at the top and scrolled down to the bottom, perhaps clicking on links to other pages on the way. Today, we have screens set to higher resolutions so that you can see more information, but the text and images appear smaller. This offers more options when it comes to layout. The first thing you should consider when you are designing your own website is what kind of 'look' you want to be associated with.

Niall Clutton shows the range of his work with three rows of thumbnails. Each small image clicks through to larger versions with slideshow buttons to move through his gallery. His homepage gets straight down to business by describing his work and providing telephone and email contact details.

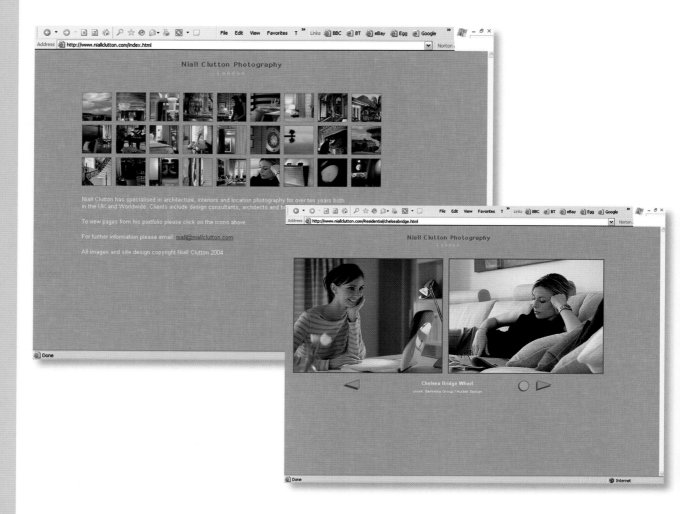

The arty look

Art photographers, especially those who specialize in tranquil landscapes and moody portraiture, might want their images to do all the communicating. A photographer who has dedicated a career to capturing the splendour of Scotland or the Sahara might like to choose an image that sums up that career and present that as the key 'look' for the website.

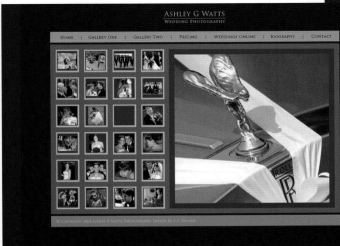

Ashley Watts's website (left and above) uses muted colours and an elegant serif font to convey a sense of refinement and distinction. The look and feel is consistent through the galleries and the rest of the site.

Johnny Greig's website design (below) is also clean and simple, but his use of a more modern typeface, powerful colour and strong shapes creates a very different look to Ashley Watts' site (above).

For this type of look, the image is everything. All other elements, such as name, contact details and career notes, will be subtle, low-key and understated. This photographer is saying to visitors: 'This photograph is the most important thing you need to know about me. I am confident that it is strong enough to speak for me. I don't want to detract from it with commercial messages. If you like my photograph, you'll get in touch.'

This minimalist approach is very cool. It has a confidence about it that some clients will like. They will see you as the kind of person that they want to be associated with; a talented artist who does not have to try very hard to win business.

There is a flip side to this approach, however. Other potential clients might see this approach as aloof, impersonal and even arrogant. It might suggest that you will be too expensive – out of their league, perhaps.

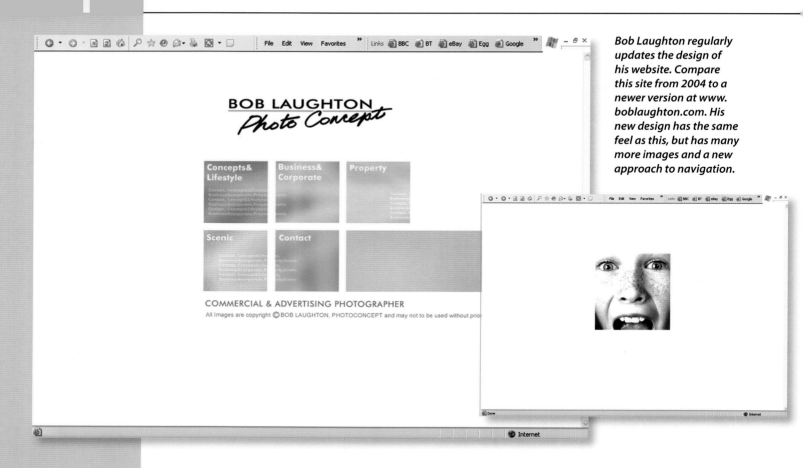

Bob Laughton regularly updates the design of his website. Compare this site from 2004 to a newer version at www. boblaughton.com. His new design has the same feel as this, but has many more images and a new approach to navigation.

The commercial look

If you want to avoid an image of being too aloof, then a more commercial site could be the answer. A commercial photographer who is taking factory interiors and product pack shots during the week and wedding pictures on Saturdays will want to demonstrate his or her versatility. The homepage should show the photographer's range as soon as it loads in the browser. A photomontage will do this, or a collection of diverse images, each linked to a gallery of similar work. The website could feature sections dedicated to the different disciplines and a list of satisfied customers complete with glowing testimonials.

This is already a busier, harder-selling look, and the homepage will quickly invite visitors to enquire about availability, day rate and additional services. This photographer is saying: 'Look at all this stuff I can do. There's this… and this… and look at these. I'm busy,

There are two distinct areas of Jesse Goff's work. His architecture photography is different enough from his 'stylistic' work to deserve its own website. Both sites are accessible from a simple contact page (below) that is also distinct from the look and feel of the two areas that it links into.

GOFF ⬤ PHOTOGRAPHY

| Architectural | Stylistic |

358 Brannan Street
San Francisco, CA 94107

Studio: 415.777.3700   Fax: 415.777.3730   web@jessegoff.com

residential   commercial

JESSE**GOFF** PHOTOGRAPHY   contact   services

Bringing your properties and markets into focus.

Jesse Goff's fashion photography site hits you hard with style and attitude. He has cleverly combined this strong image with slick, under-stated navigation.

obviously, but I'd like to work for you too, so here are four ways to get in touch. Let me know what you want and I'll find a way to do it.'

What's the flip side to this? Well, there's nothing wrong with appearing keen and enthusiastic, but you don't want to seem as if you are desperate. The cool photographer might come across as if he or she doesn't need the work and a client might be lucky to get them. The keen photographer obviously wants clients. Both approaches are good. Which one suits you?

You could try both approaches, of course. It's so easy to set up a website that you can always create two contrasting online 'brands'. As long as you have ways of monitoring the response from each, you can soon find out which method works best for you.

The ePHOTOzine website includes news, equipment reviews, techniques, discussion and galleries – so the site team (below right) are kept very busy. The result is a huge online resource and a cool place to hang out.

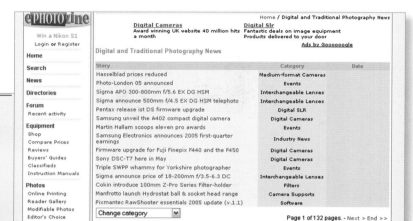

The community website

If you are less interested in getting new work from your website and more excited by the prospect of sharing your pictures with others and exchanging views about them and photography in general, your best option might be a community-driven website. Presenting your images as the focal point of discussion might be important, so a gallery of images linked to a message board for each could feature in the look of the website.

Comment from you will generate feedback, but try to keep it short. Panels and pages presenting your views on subjects like digital imaging, photo retouching and preferred equipment will help to stimulate debate. Opportunities for visitors to email you their views will be popular, as will links from each section to a message board. If you strike the right look and tone, this kind of site could become very busy, so be prepared for what it means to become the 'hub of the community'.

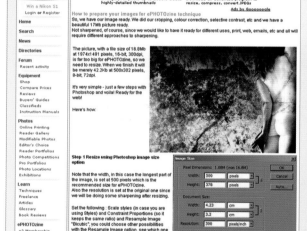

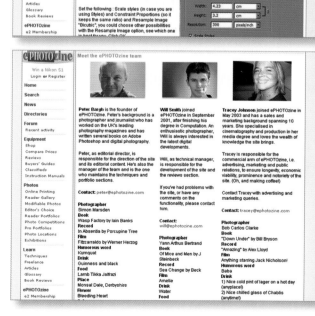

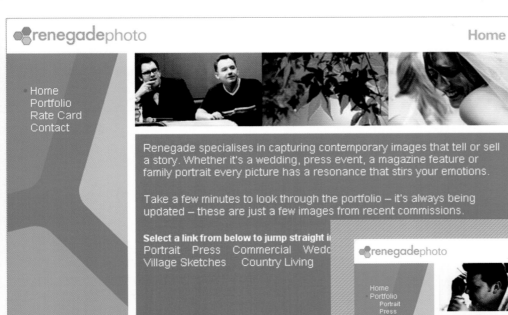

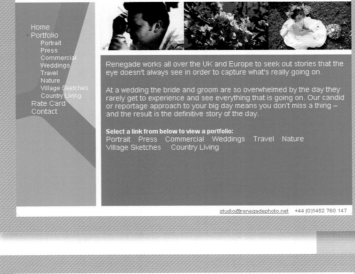

Renegade sticks to certain basic design shapes and colours throughout its site (above). The look is clean and simple rather than cool and minimalist.

Which is best for you?

So, there we have three 'looks' to consider: the cool, arty, minimalist approach; the busier, commercial, info-led presentation; and the community site, which focuses on the exchange of opinions and visitors interacting with you and each other.

The easiest type of site to create and maintain is the cool, arty site. It's simple and, once done, if it works or you just like it, you can leave it alone.

The info-laden site will take longer to create, simply because there's so much more to put on there. It will also require more maintenance, such as keeping prices up to date and adding new services and examples of work.

A community site can become an obsession. If it's successful, it can start to take over your life.

Simple web design rules

Now that you have decided on the best sort of look for your website, we can consider some of the basic rules of web design. As the power to create falls into the hands of non-experts, we are subject to some spectacularly awful results. The same thing has happened with home video, home sound recording and desktop publishing. Websites are no different, and the aim of this book is to save you from some of the most fundamental and common mistakes.

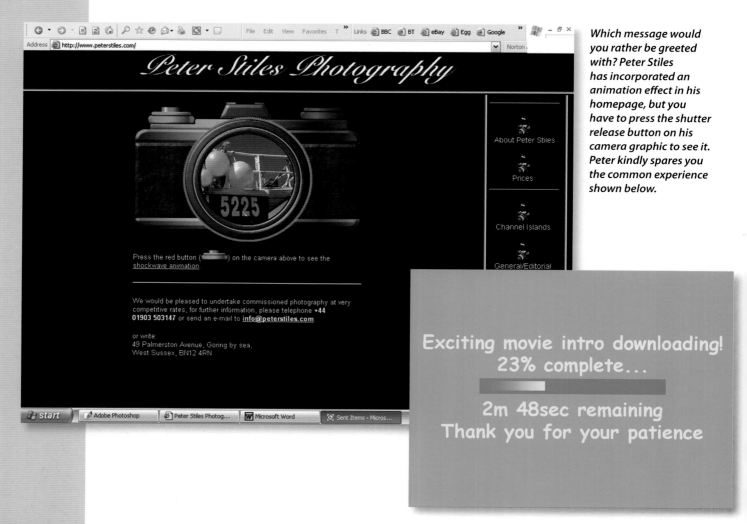

Which message would you rather be greeted with? Peter Stiles has incorporated an animation effect in his homepage, but you have to press the shutter release button on his camera graphic to see it. Peter kindly spares you the common experience shown below.

There are exceptions to every rule. If you happen to be truly brilliant, use an equally talented multimedia web designer, and want your site to feature the latest technology and presentation, your movie intros will be worth waiting for. Renowned photographers Carl De Keyzer and Martin Parr both use wonderful animated graphics on their sites.

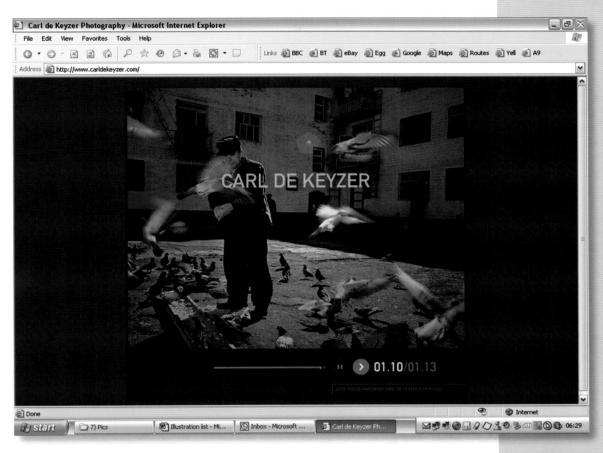

Take care with movie intros

Be wary of using long movie intros, background music and coloured text on coloured pages. They all have the potential to be very irritating.

Movie intros are still quite popular, especially on sites for big brands or media-rich sites promoting cinema films or entertainers. Interactive sites for children, too, rely on a lot of preloaded animation.

These movie intros usually greet the viewer with a message about how much of it has loaded. The viewer then has the privilege of watching the download progress, not even sure if the ensuing spectacle is something they need or want to see.

With increasing numbers of Internet users switching to broadband, and website designers finding ways to make the file sizes of movie intros smaller, this problem is diminishing. Nonetheless, the most considerate website

Tim James' site opens with his exterior architectural images, featuring a striking opener and clickable thumbnails along the bottom. His gallery of interiors follows the same layout, and the thumbnails remain in place when you move to his biography and contact pages. Tim has achieved this by using frames. Each page of the site is divided into three separate windows; the navigation frame on the left remains in view as the contents of the other windows change.

designers will include a small 'Skip intro' link in the corner of the screen that allows visitors to go straight into the site proper.

Movie intros are usually created using Flash multimedia technology, which can produce stunning animation. Just look at some of the demos on the manufacturer's website at www.macromedia.com. Flash technology offers wonderful possibilities, which are all beyond the scope of this book to explain. There is a lot of information on the Macromedia website; if you really want some Flash action, you can consider having something created for you and then built into your site just like any other graphic.

For the purposes of this book, however, we should stick to the animation possibilities offered by the GIF (.gif) file format. The GIF is a common type of web image that can be made to scroll through different frames to create a movie effect. Simple software is available to make animated GIFs and sophisticated image-editing packages have this feature built in.

Taking care with colour doesn't mean not using colour at all. Lighthouse's colour scheme is fantastic: it isn't all black type on white, but it is very clear; the colours are strong but far from garish. Enjoy it all at www.lighthousephotography.net.

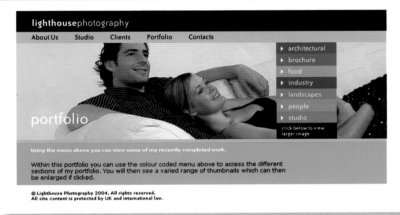

Choice of colour

Assuming that you have dropped the idea of having a movie intro, provided your visitors with a skip button, or they've endured the loading time to be thrilled by your multimedia presentation and are still with you, let's consider your proper web pages.

The look and feel that you choose for your site must be applied to every page. If you choose the same colours, typestyles and graphical layout for every page, visitors understand that they are still in the same site as they move from one page to another.

The web design rule that is most often broken is the one about colours. When it comes to type on a background, black type on a white background is the easiest to read on screen. If you simply want visitors to read your information and have any consideration for their eyesight whatsoever, you will use black type on a white background. Some designers will tell you that dark blue type on yellow is just as good, or that you can get away with a pale blue background. You might be able to get away with it, but no other colour combination is as clear as black type on a white background.

Looking around the Internet at some home-produced sites makes you wonder what people are thinking of. You see glaringly vivid colour schemes that clash and flash; there are sites with green type sitting barely legibly on a green background, and lots of people throwing around yellows and blues that are almost fluorescent! You can use colour on your website by all means, but it is best to keep it subtle, and when it comes to maximum clarity and readability, remember that simple black and white is by far the best option.

Choice of font

Choosing fonts is another important decision. When you design a web page, most programs allow you to use any of the fonts installed on your computer. But there is no guarantee that the people who will view your site have the same fonts installed on their computers, so you cannot be sure that they will see your site in the way that you intended it.

To avoid this problem, you should always choose one of the standard, 'web-safe' fonts that are installed on virtually every computer from new.

4

Times New Roman, Bold, *Italic*, *Bold Italic*
Arial, Bold, *Italic*, *Bold Italic*
Courier New, Bold, *Italic*, *Bold Italic*

Stick with these fonts and you won't go far wrong. Remember, if you use a font on a web page and a visitor doesn't have that font on their computer, they won't see what you intended them to see.

These fonts include:

• **Times New Roman, Bold, *Italic*, *Bold Italic***
This is the universal 'serif' type face. Serif means that the font has small lines at the ends of the main stroke in a character. This font is simply known as Times on Apple Macintosh computers.

• **Arial, Bold, *Italic*, *Bold Italic***
No little lines on the ends of the main strokes means that this is a 'sans serif' font. Apple computers use the almost identical Helvetica.

• **Courier New, Bold, *Italic*, *Bold Italic***
This is a serif font that looks as if it were created on an old-fashioned typewriter.

• **Verdana** and **Georgia** are also popular fonts widely used and commonly available for all computers.

When you create pages with the web editor set to 'Default font', the user will see the font they have set as the default for their own browser. You might have your default set as Arial, so that's what you'll see when you test the site. However, a user who has set Times New Roman as their browser default font will see this where you see Arial. You can override this by specifying Arial when you create your pages, which will display as Arial on all browsers. The only way to present other typestyles and be certain that viewers will see them correctly is to create them with an image-editing program that allows you to save the text in a picture format. We'll look at how to do this later (see pages 80–81).

Keeping text concise

A general rule says that you should keep any text concise. Visitors to websites tend to avoid reading pages and pages of dense copy. Try to say everything that you have to say in short, snappy sentences. Web copy tends to be written in almost note-taking style. For any unavoidably long passages, use larger type or suggest that visitors print the page and read the hard copy. But wherever possible, keep text short.

Size of web page

The final simple rule for this section is about size. Computer screens come in different sizes, and users can change the settings for their screens and affect how things appear. Screen resolution uses the pixel as its standard unit and you can choose how many pixels your computer screen displays. Nobody these days sets up their screens to show less than 800 pixels across by 600 pixels down. Most modern computers display 1024 pixels by 768 pixels.

Because there are still people using computers that have monitors with 800 x 600 resolution, we need to use this to determine the size of our web pages. If someone wants to view your web page with Internet Explorer, the most common web browser, and they have the standard set of toolbars visible, then the biggest area that they can see in the viewing window on their screen is about 780 pixels by 440 pixels. This is when the browser window is set to maximum and they are not using the side panel to search or view the history of websites that they have previously visited.

Small, dark text on a lighter background dominates the look of these three successful websites. Sans serif fonts such as Arial and Helvetica are very much the favourites. Any text that requires specific fonts for logos or branding is created using images (you can learn how to do that in chapter 7). All these sites are 780 pixels wide and are ranged to the left of the browser window. Only the content-laden BBC site has information extending below a typical screen display, requiring the visitor to scroll down.

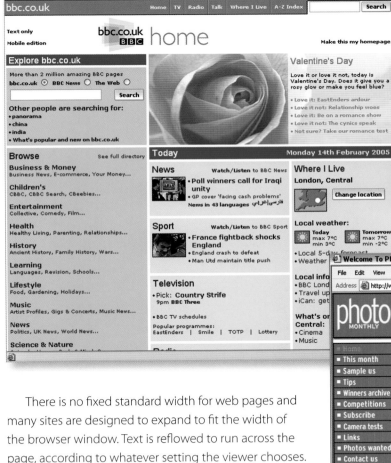

There is no fixed standard width for web pages and many sites are designed to expand to fit the width of the browser window. Text is reflowed to run across the page, according to whatever setting the viewer chooses. If a web page is designed to fit the width of the window, then images that were originally placed side by side might get pushed onto separate lines when the window is narrower than the original layout.

It has become fairly common practice now to use a set width for a web page and not to allow images and text to reflow. A quick check of a select few websites suggests that 780 pixels is a frequently used width for a web page these days.

5: Organizing your website's content

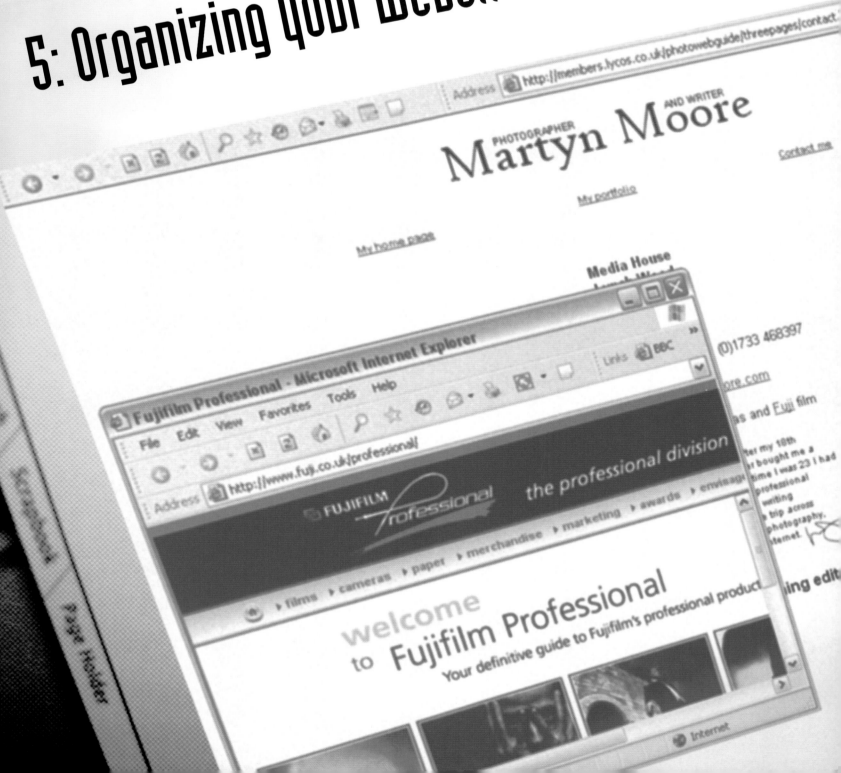

Organizing your website's content

Once you have decided roughly how your website will look, you need to plan its content and structure. Don't start feeling intimidated at this point: you don't need a fancy software program to do this; you can start off with a simple pencil-and-paper outline. Once you start organizing your materials on your computer, however, you do need to be pretty rigorous about where you put things and what you name them. You will soon find out if you do this wrong, as the links on your website won't work once it's up and running.

5 | A low-tech start

▨ **The initial planning of your website can be achieved by jotting down ideas and sketches with a pencil and paper. This is a good way of clarifying the structure and content of your website and working out exactly what you want before turning to the computer to implement your plans.**

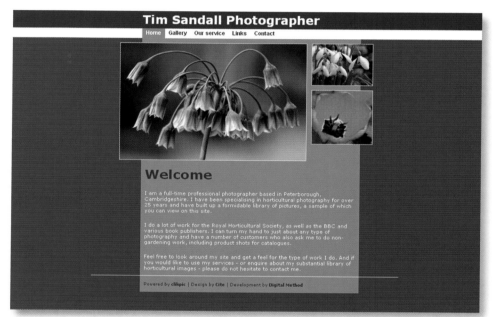

Tim Sandall's site is a good example of simple but effective presentation. His homepage is attractive and friendly, putting the visitor at ease and giving them a positive impression of what he might be like to work with. Five main sections are enough, with seven galleries. Each time the homepage (left) and the gallery page (below) are opened, different photographs are displayed – this is a nice touch.

Initial planning on paper

We're halfway through the book and guess what… it's time to start work. You are now going to create a website.

Let's look at the things you are going to need: a fast-processing PC with flat screen monitor and 80Gb of disk space? Not yet. A 500Mb webspace with FTP access and domain forwarding? You might need that soon, perhaps, but not now. No; all you need to start designing your web page is a pencil and some paper.

Create your first ideas on paper. You don't have to be Da Vinci; you're only drawing some boxes. The boxes will represent the graphics on your page. Lines of text can be written in where you know you want to say something.

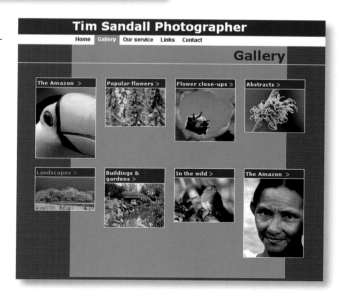

These rough sketches represent Tim Sandall's site (opposite). By transferring your ideas to paper in this way, you can try various shapes and layouts without even turning on the computer. Such sketches are essential when working with a professional web designer, too.

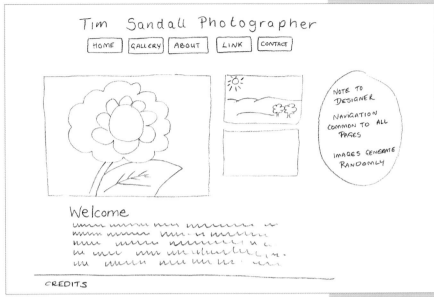

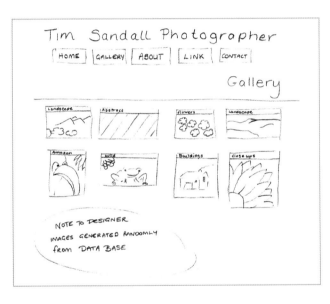

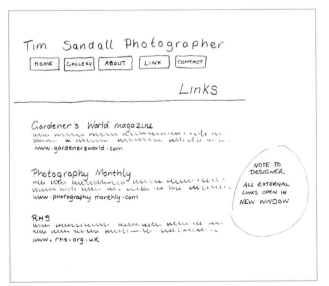

Write in the first couple of words to remind you, then degenerate into squiggly lines. For lines of text where you don't know what to say, just use squiggly lines.

The idea of this exercise is to get some sense of proportion and relative sizes. Make sure you have looked at plenty of websites first for inspiration and that you can refer back to these, borrowing layout ideas and trying them in your sketches.

When you are tired of drawing boxes and squiggly lines, stop. It would be nice at this stage to have one dominant theme coming through, but it doesn't matter yet if all you have is four sketches that seem to bear no relation to each other.

Drawing up a site plan

The next stage is to think about your site plan. Just for a change, you will be drawing boxes and straight lines this time. The boxes will represent pages on your site and the straight lines will be the links between the pages.

Some clever web design software has automated this process and allows you to create the site plan on your computer. It will even create the basic pages as you draw the boxes, and put automatic links to other pages that modify themselves as you add and delete boxes. By all means use this technology if it suits your way of working. Instructions and guides to get you started will be included with whatever software you choose, probably as part of the 'Help' section.

Otherwise, just start by drawing a box to represent the homepage. You can put this at the top of your sheet of paper or right in the middle. If you start at the top, the site map will tend to cascade down like a family tree. Site maps with the homepage in the centre end up looking like a mind-mapping exercise. Choose the style you like the sound of. Many site maps are wider than they are deep, so consider which way you orient your sheet – landscape might be best.

Imagine somebody arriving at your homepage. Now try to think of all the sections you would like them to click off into. The simplest, three-page website will tell your visitors all about you on the homepage; it will have a contact page with all your details and maybe an email link and then perhaps a page showing a small selection of your work.

The homepage will have a link to both of the other pages, and both of the other pages must have a link to the homepage. Draw little arrowheads on your lines to show which way the link goes.

Linking pages

With such a small site, it's very easy to link the other pages too, so visitors can click to the portfolio section from the contact page and vice versa. Get into the habit of drawing all these links in.

Now imagine that there are three photos on the page where you show samples of your work, and you would like to show bigger versions of each picture on its own page. This is adding three new pages to your website, all coming off the portfolio page.

When you make the pages, you can decide whether the links on them should open the next page in the same browser window, or whether they open up a new additional browser window.

This simple site plan represents the structure of many basic websites. Starting with the homepage at the top, the sections and pages cascade down much like a family tree. Try to keep layout information separate (see previous page) and concentrate on navigation.

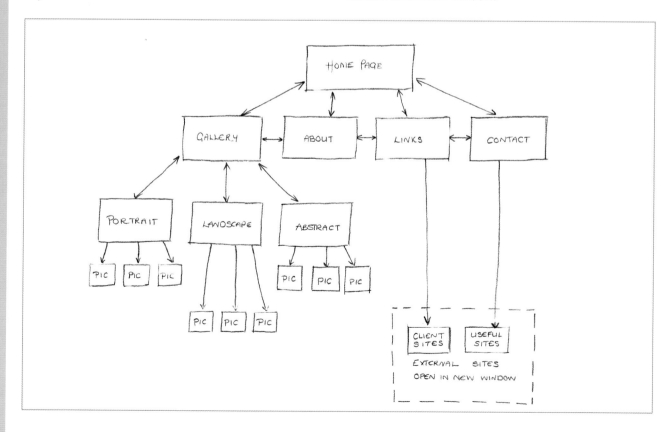

If you go to this site and click the links to internal pages – My home page, My portfolio and Contact me – the new page opens in the same window in place of the page you click from (right). However, if you click the links to external sites – Nikon and Fuji – the new pages open in a new window on top of the page you click from (below right). This helps visitors stay on your site, which remains open in the background.

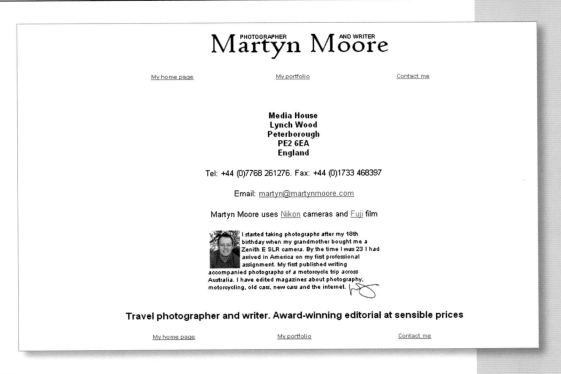

The rule of thumb for this is: if the next page is within your own website, it's normal to open it in the same window. However, if you have linked to an external website – somebody else's site – then this page would open in a new window.

The benefit of this is that although visitors are opening up a page on another website, they haven't left your site, which is still sitting open in a window underneath the new page.

With the three pages of photographs you are adding to your site, you can either create them in a new window, or let them replace the portfolio page in the existing window. If you use the same window, you will need to provide a link back to the portfolio page, or a 'Back' link, on each page. If you open the separate photos in new windows, you don't need the link back, but you should provide a button that will close the window. Without this, the viewer will end up with lots of open windows, all on top of each other. This can be confusing and irritating.

Scripts to close windows are available on the website at www.websitesforphotographers.co.uk. They are simple commands that are inserted into the code of the web page where a graphical button is used.

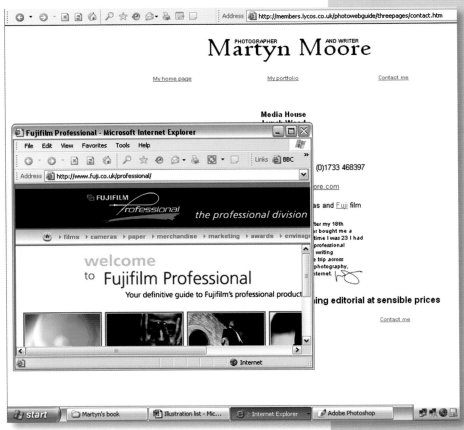

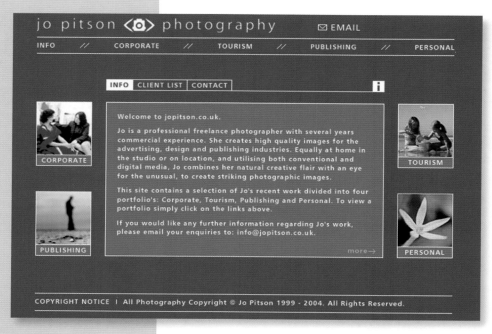

Jo Pitson's site, designed by doodlebox.co.uk, is clean and clear. It shows you everything you need to know on the homepage and provides obvious entry points to areas with more detailed information.

Planning galleries

By creating three new pages with bigger photographs, and accessing them from smaller thumbnail pictures collected on the portfolio page, you have actually created a rudimentary gallery function. The gallery is a very useful device for photographers' websites. By providing the right kind of navigation, and using a logical file-naming convention, it is possible to create a very effective gallery of your pictures.

The concept is quite simple: your website has a portfolio page on it that displays a dozen small versions of images known as thumbnails. If a visitor clicks on any of these images, a bigger version of the image they clicked will appear. Navigation links or buttons in that window will then allow visitors to view a large version of the next image in the portfolio, without going back to the page of thumbnails. The links can also be set up to allow the selection of individual images, or to view the previous image in the sequence as well as the next one. A link back to the thumbnails page appears on each gallery page, too.

Because gallery sections are so useful, we have created two different styles for you on the website at www.websitesforphotographers.co.uk. They all work on the same principle and all contain a set of instructions on how to incorporate them into your own website. They

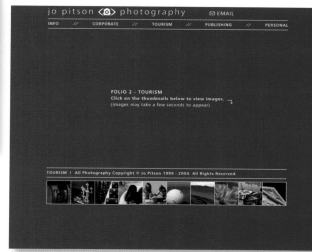

Chris Nash divides his work into disciplines for his galleries, but his great skill as a dance photographer is still evident in his commercial and fashion work.

The navigation for Ronnie Israel's London portfolio is inspired by the River Thames.

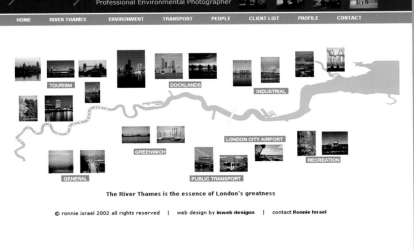

can easily be customized and we strongly recommend that you download one and have a play.

Following the instructions of a web gallery will give you a clear understanding of some of the principles of good web design. The logic behind links and the need for consistent image formatting are key to an effective gallery. The names you give to files and the folders they are stored in are also vital.

You have to be organized and disciplined if you don't want to spend your life tracking down missing files and broken navigation links. So that's what we're going to do next – get organized.

Organizing your material

It is important to organize all the materials that you need for your website on your computer. Create your folders and pay attention to what you put in them and where you place them. If you don't do this, you run the risk of having links that don't work when your website is up and running.

HTML code is what holds a web page together. The web design software usually generates it automatically, so you don't really need to know it. However, it might help to be familiar with it. You can see the HTML code in a web page by going to the View menu in Internet Explorer and choosing Source. The code opens up as text in Notepad on a PC. In the code shown here, you can see the page text; the image is called 'montage. jpg' and it links to a page called 'gallery.html'.

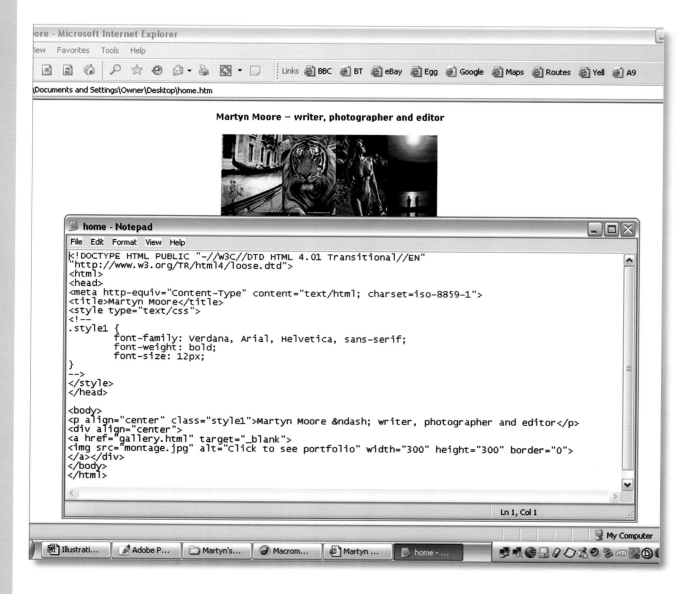

The importance of being organized

Are you methodical and organized? Do you have a place for everything and is everything in its place? If not, web design may not be for you.

The way in which HTML, the code behind what you see on a web page, works is by calling up pictures and graphics and displaying them in relation to text that forms part of the code itself. This means that most of the words are part of the HTML and the images are drawn onto the page by having links to them.

These images can be on the same computer as the pages, or they can be in the same set of folders, or in the same folder. The images can also be in different folders, on a different computer, or even on a different website altogether. What is important is that you know where the images are and that the page code can find them.

More problems are caused by wrong image links than almost anything else, and the only way to reduce the errors is by being well organized.

Organizing folders

First of all, you need to create a folder for all the work that you are going to do on the website. If you are working on only one project, then a folder called 'My Website' in the 'My Documents' section of your computer's hard drive would make a lot of sense. Everything you do should happen in this folder.

The next folder you create could be called 'Raw Images'. This is where you can store digital photos, scans and graphics at their original size and resolution. Often these files will be too large for use on your website. You can also do the same with 'Raw Text' by storing all the words for the site as Word or text (.txt) documents. Keeping all original text and images is a very sensible thing to do, as information can be lost along the way. It is a useful insurance policy and can save time if something goes wrong.

Now create a folder called something like 'Publish' or 'To Live Site'. This is the most important folder of

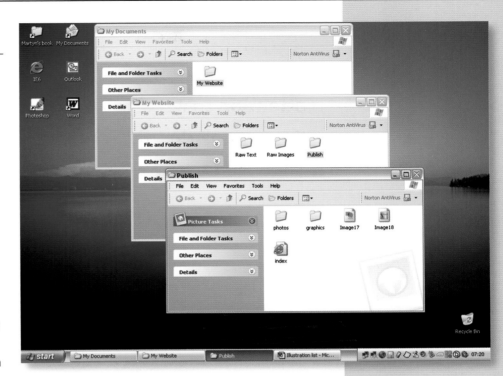

all, because the contents of this folder should exactly replicate the contents of the live site folder on your web server. If it doesn't, you will start to get errors and missing links to pictures and graphics.

Two more folders can be created within your Publish folder: one for graphics that are used as page furniture (buttons, icons, logos and the like), and one for the photographs you will use on your site. Call them 'Graphics' and 'Photos'. These folders will contain all your web-ready images; they will be cropped, formatted and compressed to exactly the right spec for use on your pages and saved to these folders. When you start to build your pages, you will call them up from these folders. This is important.

The web pages themselves will sit in your Publish folder, outside your graphics folders. Eventually, you might start to create new website sections that have their own folders with graphics folders within the Publish folder. A set of gallery pages, for example, might be entirely nested within Publish with its own folder and graphics folders. Just make sure that you keep the relative locations of folders, pages and graphics constant, otherwise links will be broken.

All neat, tidy and ordered. The top window shows the Publish folder – home of the final versions of everything to be posted on the site. The Publish folder lives in My Website, which contains all the raw materials that have been processed. This is the Publish folder for a site created with a word processor, so copies of images have been created outside the photos and graphics folder. Normally they would be inside these folders. This is explained in detail in Chapter 7.

This site was created without the help of a web wizard. Each page was created individually and all the graphics were dumped in a single folder with the HTML documents. There's an index page in there somewhere – but it works!

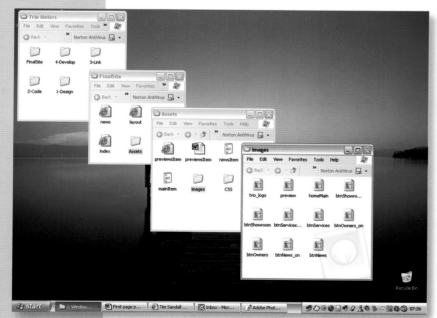

When creating a series of web pages using Dreamweaver, the pages and all their assets can be automatically placed in a folder structure with a logical hierarchy. The Trio Motors folder shows all the stages of the Dreamweaver tutorial.

Looking after links

Let's imagine that you have created a simple three-page website and now want to add a gallery. You created your gallery using a template that you downloaded from www.websitesforphotographers.co.uk and you did all your work on your computer desktop. If you created a link to that gallery on your existing homepage before you moved the new gallery into your Publish folder, the link will be broken when you do move it. The homepage link will still be looking on the desktop.

The same thing applies when it comes to images. If you create a page in Publish and insert an image, that image must be the final web-ready formatted version and must be placed in the appropriate graphics folder, also in Publish. Moving files and changing names after pages have been created will result in missing files and broken links on your website.

To be honest, it won't kill you if this sort of error happens to you once or twice. The process of solving the problem and fixing the link will help you to understand how everything works and the importance of being organized.

Many of the popular web-building programs create a folder structure for you, especially if you use the Microsoft-style 'wizards', which take you through the processes step by step. Microsoft's FrontPage, part of Office, will do this, and Macromedia's applications include file and folder management. This is all very helpful and provides a very non-technical process.

However, the more automated the process, the less you will understand it. It has already been stated that the purpose of this book is not to turn you into a professional website builder or a computer geek, but if you spend a little bit of time grasping the basics it will pay off in the long run.

A summary

Let us have a quick look at what you have achieved so far. You have a clear idea of what you would like your website to do, and you have thought about how you would like it to look. You should have had a go at drawing up a simple site plan, showing your homepage and the links to and from the other pages on your site and maybe to some external websites.

And now you have created the folders and working areas on your own computer. Let's assume that your computer has an image-editing program. PCs using the Windows operating system have an application called Paint. It is not as smart as Photoshop or Paint Shop Pro, but it is enough to get started.

Your computer will have word-processing software. If it is a Windows-based PC, this will be part of Microsoft Works – the simplest word processor that comes preloaded on almost all machines. Works Word Processor can save documents as HTML – a web page.

So, that's it. We can't put it off any longer. We are well prepared and have our material organized, so now we are going to create our very first web page using the tools that come as standard on most home computers.

Dreamweaver's site, link and navigation management appears on the right-hand side of the workspace.

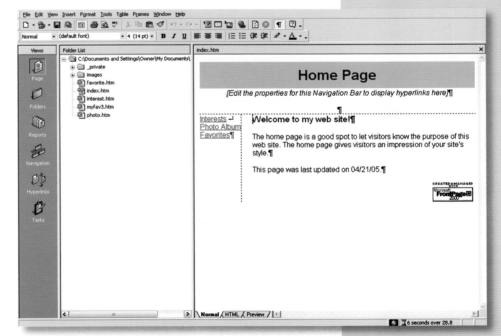

Microsoft's FrontPage creates linked web pages that can be managed via the panels on the left of the screen. Navigation and links can be created and maintained automatically across all pages on the site.

6: Optimizing images for the web

Optimizing images for the web

Preparing images to be published on the web involves practices that might seem antithetical to a photographer used to optimizing image quality. You have to make sure that your images are small enough for your viewers to download before they run out of patience. You also need to make sure that they are at the appropriate resolution to appear on computer screens, and you need to consider what format to save your image files in. This chapter takes you step by step through the methods of optimizing your images.

6 Preparing photos for your site

> Before you upload any images to your website, you will need to optimize them for the web first. You will have to bear in mind issues such as file size, resolution, image size and file format. Remember that not all your website visitors will have a broadband connection and you cannot expect them to sit happily for hours waiting for your images to appear on their desktops.

Image quality and file size

The aims of the photographer and the requirements of an efficient website often seem at odds. The good photographer lives in pursuit of the ultimate image quality. Back in the days when film and projection printing were the only options, a photographer would choose film with the finest possible grain to create the sharpest, most detailed pictures. Hours spent in the darkroom would result in huge prints with extraordinary ranges of tone and hue.

Converting these images into digital files or creating digital images of a similar quality consumes enormous amounts of computer memory. The bigger the image and the more detail you want to show in the print, the bigger the digital file size.

To give you some idea of the file sizes involved, a full-page photograph in this book would create a file size of about 50 to 100Mb on a computer. The factors that govern file size are actual image size, image resolution (the size and number of dots that make up the image), and the depth of colour (or the number of shades).

A full-page image in this book measures approximately 260 x 240mm (10¼ x 9½in). The resolution the printer works to is about 300dpi – that's about 300 dots to every linear inch, or 90,000 dots in every square inch of the picture. The colour is made up of varying percentages of cyan, magenta, yellow and black, while the white is the colour of the paper. That is quite a lot of information to hold in one image file.

A printed book page is not a particularly high-quality image, either. For images to rival those that are created in a darkroom on photographic paper, the resolution needs to be at least four times more fine. This means that 1200dpi only just starts to rival the quality obtained using traditional photography methods. In a high-end digital imaging laboratory, file sizes in excess of 500Mb are a day-to-day reality; enormous computing power is required to handle and manipulate images of this size.

For our purposes, though, we should stick to the example of a full-page picture in this book. An image like that can be managed on a normal home computer fairly easily. It is the type of image that you might create yourself with a desktop scanner or a professional-specification digital camera.

This digital image is no good for use on the web, however; it's far too big. When an image is placed on a web page, the viewer has to download the digital file from the Internet in order to see it on a computer screen. Despite the popularity of broadband – high-speed Internet access – many Internet users still use modems on a phone line that dials another modem and exchanges information at a rate of less than 56kbps (56,000 bytes per second). A 50Mb file has 50,000,000 bytes in it, so even on

An image like this, reproduced large on the printed page, might use up more than 50Mb of computer memory.

a good day the smallest of our full-page image files would take fifteen minutes to download. In reality though, 56k modems often run as slow as 20kbps. People would die of starvation waiting for a photograph to appear.

Not only is the file size impossible to accommodate on a web page for practical reasons; it's inappropriate for aesthetic reasons, too. A computer screen displays images at a resolution of 72dpi, irrespective of the actual resolution of that image. So when you look at a photograph that has been scanned at 300dpi, you only see 72dpi on the screen. For screen use, most of the image information in a 300dpi digital image is redundant. It simply can't be seen.

For these reasons, you should look to reduce the file size of any of the images that you intend to place on your website.

These are details of large (approximately 300mm high) scans made at high resolution (300dpi) from 35mm transparencies. They are ideal at this size for good-quality printing in a book or magazine, but are far too big to use on the web.

Reducing image file size

When you create image files for a website, the first place you should look to reduce file size is resolution. All images that are intended for screen use should be no more than 72dpi. Therefore, if you are scanning a print for use on your website, you should set the scanner settings to create a 72dpi-resolution image file. However, you are more likely to be dealing with existing digital files: scans that you have made to copy prints or the files from a digital camera. These files are probably at a higher resolution than you require, and you therefore need to reduce the number of dots per inch to 72.

With very basic image-editing software and resizing tools, when you change a 150dpi image to 72dpi, the image dimensions or print size are simply doubled and you end up with the same file size and image information expressed in a different way. You need to use an image-editing program that resamples the image and allows you to adjust the dimensions of the image in pixels or linear measurement units (millimetres or inches, for example) as well as the resolution of the image in dots per inch.

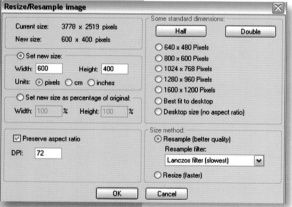

With the free (for home use) image editor IrfanView, resizing and resampling images is simple. This screengrab shows the various options for reducing the image size and resolution to web-friendly proportions, all in one comprehensive control panel.

Another very useful feature of more sophisticated image-editing software is the ability to maintain the aspect ratio of an image. That is, it will keep the image in proportion when you change just one of the measurements. Let's imagine, for example you are working with an image that is 600 pixels wide by 400 pixels high. If you want to use the image at half that width, a good image editor will allow you to change the width of the image to 300 pixels and then automatically change the height to 200 pixels for you.

Of course, with numbers like that, you can do the calculation in your head. However, imagine that you have an image that is 729 pixels by 488 pixels and you want to use it 371 pixels wide – try working out that height in your head. Obviously, it is much easier if you can just click the box that says 'Preserve aspect ratio' or 'Constrain proportions'.

Therefore, you will see that it is essential to have image-editing software that can resample an image and

When saving as a JPEG, the IrfanView software provides a slider to adjust the degree of compression. Lower compression gives better quality images; higher compression reduces quality.

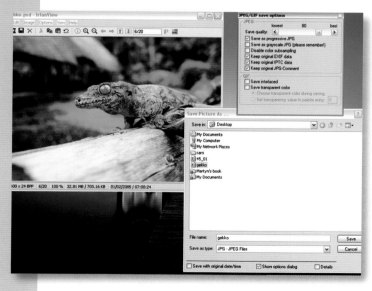

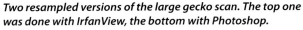
Two resampled versions of the large gecko scan. The top one was done with IrfanView, the bottom with Photoshop.

allow you to convert it to the ideal screen resolution of 72dpi. Software that will also allow you to resize an image and keep the shape in proportion is highly desirable. As it happens, a free image-editing package that does just these things is provided for you on the website at www.websitesforphotographers.co.uk. Download it now and experiment with it.

You might notice, as you try different image-editing programs, that the results from each can be slightly different. You can see from the pictures of the gecko reproduced above that different programs can create different colour effects. No adjustment was made to the colours in either of these pictures, but the difference between the resulting image files is quite marked.

Size of images and aspect ratios

Another thing to take into consideration is the size of the images that you intend to use on your website. It is quite common, for example, for smaller images, such as thumbnails that link to a bigger display version of an image, to be 100 pixels wide or less. Display versions of images are commonly 200 to 300 pixels wide, and these pictures dominate a web page. The biggest images you are likely to display are the ones you provide as desktop wallpaper for visitors to download. These will be either 800 or 1024 pixels wide, but the design of the web page might prevent all of the bigger image size from being viewed. The latest versions of common web browsers like Internet Explorer will fit a huge image into their viewing windows, but if you design your pages properly this shouldn't be necessary.

Earlier in the book we looked at consistency in design and image sizes. If you choose two or three standard

Both resampled images are shown open in Photoshop. You can see that the colours have been boosted in the IrfanView version (gekkoIF.jpg). The Photoshop version (gekkoPS.jpg) is more natural and the finished file size is bigger than the IrfanView. The greater power of Photoshop would allow you to replicate the IrfanView effect if you wanted to.

image sizes and then stick with them throughout the site, your pages will have a more coherent look.

It might be easier if you base your preferred image sizes on normal photographic aspect ratios, such as 3:2 for 35mm film. This could lead you to choose 80 pixels by 54 pixels for your tiniest thumbnails, 160 pixels by 108 pixels for your medium-sized display images, and 640 pixels by 432 pixels for the largest versions of images in your gallery.

Digital images come in all shapes and sizes. Pictures that have been produced with a digital camera might be created using the 4:3 proportions of a standard computer screen: 800 pixels by 600 pixels or 1024 pixels by 768 pixels. A 10 x 8in print will produce a scan that is 720 pixels by 576 pixels if set to a screen resolution of 72dpi. An A4-sized image in portrait, or upright, format (210mm x 297mm/8¼ x 11¾in) will result in an image that is 595 pixels by 842 pixels.

If you have decided to base your image sizes throughout your website on the 3:2 ratio, then pictures that don't conform to those proportions will have to be cropped. The alternative is to set the width of all images and allow the depths to be whatever the image-editing package's 'constrain proportions' feature dictates, so picture height will be allowed to vary.

Cropping is very simple, however, and although many photographers frown on the practice, changing a composition using a photo-editing program has put right many mistakes made with the camera.

If you use the photo-editing program suggested on the website that accompanies this book, this allows you to open an image and then set the exact size of a selection from within that image.

So you open the picture, choose 'create custom selection' under the Edit menu and then key in the dimensions of the image you want to create. The resulting selection frame can then be moved around the full-size image until a satisfactory crop appears in the frame.

To move the frame, you need to right-click on it with the mouse. When you have the selection you want in the frame, copy the selection and use it to create your new image using Paste or Save As… from the clipboard.

Step by Step cropping a picture

1 Here we see a large scan from a 35mm transparency open in IrfanView, the free image-editing software. We want to crop into the little girl's face and get rid of the distracting window frame and side of the bus. The picture was a grabbed shot from the top of one bus to another in Hong Kong.

2 Click on the File menu and choose Create custom selection …

3 This control panel allows you to specify the size and position of the crop you want to make. The software suggests some common image sizes for you, but we have specified the size we want – 600 x 400 pixels. It is not necessary to specify the position of the selection at this stage, so ignore the X- and Y-Coordinates boxes.

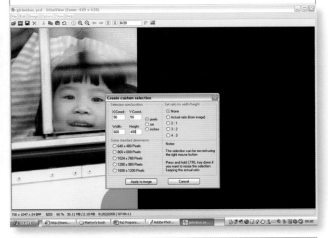

5 As soon as you are happy with the size and position of your Custom selection, you can copy the contents of the frame using either the Edit menu, the Copy button or Ctrl+C keys. This image shows the selection copied to the clipboard.

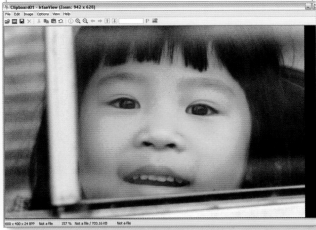

4 With the selection created and defined by a rectangular frame, you can position it wherever you want on the original image. To move the frame around, all you have to do is right-click on it with the mouse and drag it where you want it. To change the size of the frame, press the Ctrl key and drag a corner of the box; this will keep the aspect ratio constant.

6 From the clipboard, the cropped image can either be saved as a new image or pasted into another image. Choose Save As… to give you the option of creating a web-friendly JPEG file and adjusting the amount of compression for a small file size without losing too much quality.

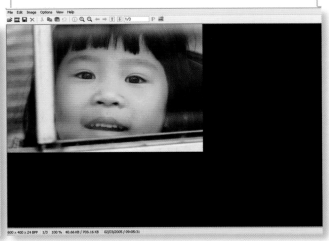

6

Working with layers

One of the great features of Photoshop, the most widely used image-editing software among professionals, is the ability to work with layers of images. A picture created or modified in Photoshop can consist of a 'background', which can be transparent or of any colour you like, and then a series of layers sitting on top of that background. Imagine these layers as clear sheets with image elements on them, all laid one on top of the other. Layers can cover part or all of the background and individual layers can be edited and adjusted independently.

The layers feature can be used to crop a larger image to your preferred width and height. In the example shown on these pages, we are going to make a landscape-format 72dpi image that will be 640 pixels wide using a portrait-format 304dpi image that is 2506 pixels wide.

In this step-by-step guide you will see how the layers facility in Photoshop can be used to crop an image. We create a new file at the size we want and then move an image layer around in its window to get the desired crop. Again, we start with a high-resolution scan from a 35mm transparency.

1 Cut down the image file size by changing the resolution from 304dpi to 72dpi in the Image Size section of Photoshop's Image menu. Without clicking OK, also change the width in pixels (not print size) to 700 – slightly wider than the desired crop. Make sure the Resample Image box is checked and click OK.

2 Now open up a new image file and set its size to the exact dimensions and image resolution of the desired crop. This will open up with a plain background, usually white, black or transparent. You can define the background when you create the new file, but for this task it doesn't matter.

3 Go back to the original image, still open next to your new file. Click on it to make it active and press Ctrl+A. This will select the whole image. Now press Ctrl+C. This will copy the whole image.

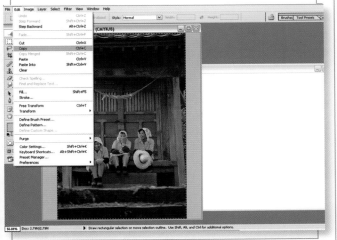

5 By selecting the 'mover' tool from the Toolbar, you can use the mouse to slide the layer over the background, moving the part of the image you want into the viewable area.

4 Click back on the new file to make that active and press Ctrl+V. This will paste the large image onto the background of your new file as a layer. You will see how the size of the layer is much bigger than the viewable area of the new file. You can see only part of the bigger image.

6 Take some time to get the exact crop that you want. When you're happy, you can then use the Save As… command to create the smaller image, cropped just the way you want it.

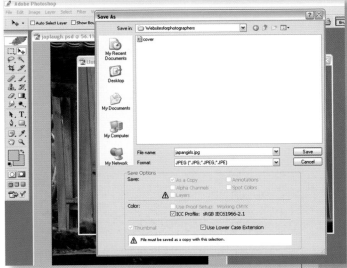

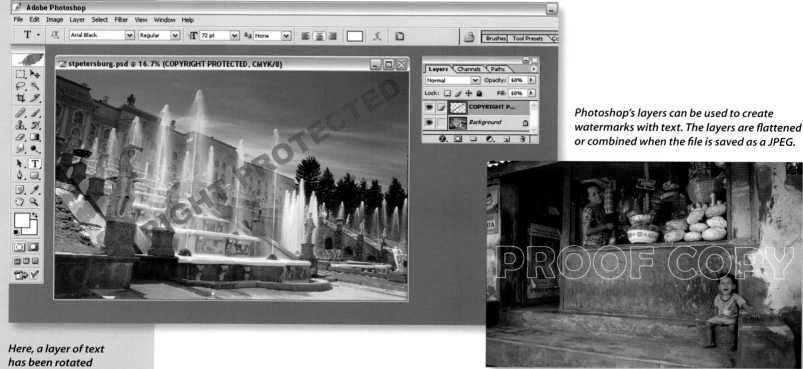

Photoshop's layers can be used to create watermarks with text. The layers are flattened or combined when the file is saved as a JPEG.

Here, a layer of text has been rotated to cross the image diagonally and the Opacity and Fill adjusted to allow the original image to show through. You can see the layer information in the panel to the right of the main image.

Combining layers and text

The layers in Photoshop are useful for lots of web applications. If you really get into the program and study all its features, entire image-rich web pages can be created. Most of that work extends beyond the range of this book, and the software evolves so quickly that you are better off using the web and dedicated publications to find out about the latest developments.

There is, however, one area of Photoshop that we can touch on here. Combine the layers feature with the text tool and you can create all your web page graphics and buttons in Photoshop. The trick is to create the bars, blocks, buttons and panels and then add text on its own layer before saving the final version of the image. That way you only create the button once but make lots of different versions using the Save As… command.

Text on its own layer is also a good way of creating the watermark effect to protect your images from misuse by others (see page 14). Experiment with different fonts and sizes on the text layer. If you choose white text, you can

then adjust the opacity of the layer to allow the original picture to show through. Special-effects filters under the Filter menu allow you to see how it might look embossed onto the image. The use of outline-style text will allow more of the image to be viewed and still provide protection against copying.

A word of warning, though: Photoshop, Paint Shop Pro, Corel Draw and many other image-editing programs are dangerously addictive.

GIFs and JPEGs

Once you have mastered the techniques of adjusting image resolution and setting the display size of all your images, the only other way of controlling the file size of your digital images is with your choice of format. The two most common types of image file in use on the web are the GIF (.gif) and the JPEG (.jpg).

GIF stands for Graphics Interchange Format. It offers the smallest file sizes for web page graphics. However, it also offers lower quality than the JPEG and is really most suitable for simple graphics like buttons, bars, panels, logos and advertising banners. The format also allows the display of a series of 'frames' – a sequence of images that creates an animation effect rather like a flip-book. There are GIF animators available from the website at www.websitesforphotographers.co.uk.

JPEG stands for Joint Photographic Experts Group, for it was they who devised this file format to display high-quality images with relatively small file sizes. This is the standard format for web images, images for attachment to emails and even the standard image format for digital cameras because of its ability to handle excellent quality.

The JPEG uses image compression to reduce the amount of memory required to make up a picture. The compression works by comparing each pixel in the image with the one next to it in every direction. If the density and hue is almost identical, then the format considers it to be the same and replicates it, effectively reducing the amount of information held in the file.

The degree of difference between adjacent pixels before they are considered the same can be adjusted, allowing you to save a JPEG at different rates of compression. When you choose the JPEG format to save an image, most image-editing programs will ask you to select a quality setting. According to the software you are using, this will be expressed as a numerical value (1–10, 1–12) or a descriptive term (low, medium, or high quality; minimum, medium, or maximum file size). Medium settings offer the best compromise between image quality and download time, but some images compress better than others, so it's worth experimenting.

JPEG compression is known as a 'lossy' form of compression. This means that each time an image is saved as a JPEG image, information is lost forever. It can never be recovered, so you should avoid resaving copies of JPEG images as each new version suffers a reduction in quality. Leave your conversion to a JPEG until the final Save As… if possible.

Perhaps predictably, image compression that preserves information is called 'lossless' compression. TIFF (.tif) and Photoshop's PSD (.psd) formats are examples of lossless compression.

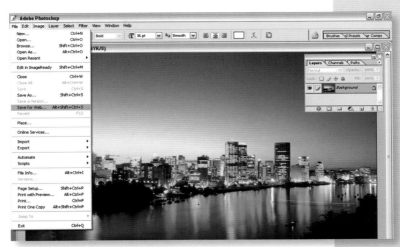

Photoshop CS users have the luxury of ImageReady to prepare photos for the web.

Save for Web command

When it comes to optimizing images for the web, users of recent versions of Photoshop have it handed to them on a plate. Any image edited in Photoshop can be exported into Adobe's Image Ready program by using the Save for Web… command.

Image Ready's main purpose is to allow the optimization of any image for use on the web. It presents tiled preview windows showing the effect on the image of different file formats, colour palettes and compression settings. Resizing and resampling can all be done from the control panel on the right.

By choosing the Save for Web… command, a large, high-resolution image is exported into ImageReady, which gives all the web-friendly file options presented side-by-side. All you have to do is choose.

7: Creating a one-page website

7:

Creating a one-page website

Having your own website does not need to be a complicated and expensive affair: a simple, one-page site can do a lot to promote your business and show off your work. You could include your company logo, a representative sample of your photography, and your contact details. This section takes you step by step through the process for creating such a site and what you need to do to upload it on to the Internet. We also look at some of the most common problems and provide some troubleshooting hints.

7 The all-important first page

■ **A one-page website is sufficient to introduce you to your Internet audience, show your work and provide contact details. Below, we take you through the step-by-step processes to creating a logo, building your web page, and uploading it to your website.**

Creating a logo

You may already have a logo. If you have been operating as a business already, you will probably have some form of corporate identity in the form of a business card or letterhead, a brochure or a catalogue. It would really help if any type styles, fonts, or distinctive imagery that are already used in your business identity are available on your computer. You can then incorporate these into the design of your website to create an aesthetically integrated business identity.

Maybe as an image person, you already have a digital version of a logo. If so, put a copy of that into the folder you've called Raw Images. If you haven't got a business or personal logo, you can make one very easily. How to achieve this is explained below.

Step by Step creating a logo

1 First of all, open Paint. You can find it under All Programs/Accessories on a PC running on Microsoft Windows. It will have opened a new image file for you. From the Image menu, choose Attributes and set the size of the new image to 468 pixels wide by 60 pixels deep.

This is a useful image size to remember, as it is the standard size of an advertising banner used across the top of many web pages. Creating design elements for your web page that follow established size and layout conventions makes it easier to create an ordered, symmetrical or balanced design when incorporating advertising elements. We're going to use it as a banner, though – we're not going to use it to make our logo.

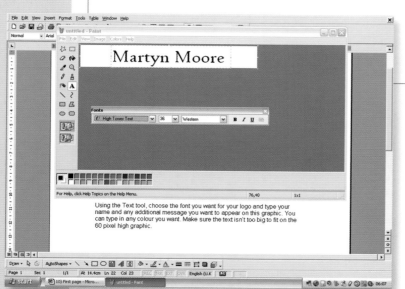

Using the Text tool, choose the font you want for your logo and type your name and any additional message you want to appear on this graphic. You can type in any colour you want. Make sure the text isn't too big to fit on the 60 pixel high graphic.

2 Using the Text tool, choose the font you want for your logo and type your name and any additional message you want to appear on this graphic. You can type in any colour you want. Make sure the text isn't too big to fit on the 60-pixel-high graphic. Paint is a quirky little program, so you might need to practise before you can get just what you want. The more sophisticated image-editing programs like Photoshop are much more powerful and user-friendly, but persevere with Paint for now.

Step by Step creating a logo (cont.)

3 When you have created the graphic you want to use as a logo, choose the Save As option from the File menu and call it 'logo'. Now save it as a GIF file into the graphics folder inside the Publish folder in My Website (as explained earlier; see pages 76–77). A GIF file is an image format that is suitable for simple graphics on a web page. It uses a limited range of colours and a resolution of 72 pixels per inch (ppi), making it perfect for quick viewing in a browser.

The GIF file format is quite exciting. With a GIF generator you can create simple animations using a series of images. The GIF format scrolls through these images creating movement or causing elements to appear and disappear, as with flick cards or a flick book. There is a simple animated GIF generator available for download at www.websitesforphotographers.co.uk and the most sophisticated image editors allow you to create animated images. Experiment with animated GIFs later. It's great fun.

Step by Step creating graphics and an image

1 Find one great image that you would like to represent your work. It doesn't have to be your greatest photo ever, but it should show the world how talented you are. If you already have a scan, or any other digital version of that photo, put a copy of that file into the folder called Raw Images in your My Website folder.

3 Now, open your photo in Raw Images and convert it to a 72dpi JPEG file that is about 600 pixels wide. Remember, 72dpi is the resolution, or 'grain size', of the image. A JPEG file is a compressed image format preferred for displaying photographs on the web, and 600 pixels is a decent width for a single image on a page. Use your image-editing software to set the resolution and width.

2 Now you really do need an image-editing tool. As a photographer ready to venture online you almost certainly have one already. Your scanner was probably supplied with an image editor and if you have a digital camera, that came with one too. The state-of-the-art image editor is Photoshop. It is expensive, but if you really get into advanced digital imaging you should consider investing in it. Paint Shop Pro is also very good – some say it is as good as Photoshop, especially when you consider its lower price. However, Microsoft Paint isn't sophisticated enough to optimize your photos for the web, so if you think that is the only image editor you have, download the free one we've posted on the website at www.websitesforphotographers.co.uk.

4 Next, choose Save As to save the file as a JPEG with a suitable name in the 'photos' folder in Publish. When the image editor asks you how much you want to compress the JPEG, pick setting four or five – 'medium' compression. It's really important to keep image file sizes as small as possible. Photography sites tend to be very rich in graphics, and although half the human race might now have access to the Internet, not everybody has broadband, so download speed is still a major consideration. Having lots of big pictures with fat file sizes will make your site slow and irritating.

Building a web page

Now, at last, you have everything in place to build your web page. Just to show you how easy it is, we are going to build it in the simple word processor found preinstalled on most Microsoft-based PCs: the Microsoft Works Word Processor.

In the chapter on organizing content (see pages 62–65), we placed images in dedicated folders. A word processing program does not know that we are smart enough to do that and therefore makes its own copy of any image we insert into the page and saves it with the page. This has been included to confuse you – proper web editors don't do this.

Step by Step building a web page

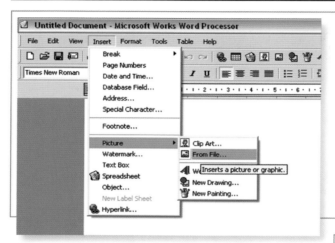

1 Open Microsoft Works Word Processor. With a blank document open, go to the Insert menu and choose Picture, then From File, or just click on the Insert Picture icon on the toolbar.

Work through the windows until you get to your graphics folder in the Publish folder of My Website. Highlight the GIF file you called 'logo' and click Insert. Your logo file should now appear on the page. Deselect the logo by clicking the right arrow direction key once and then hit return. Your cursor will move down one line.

2 Repeat the above process, only this time go to the photos folder and insert the 600 pixel-wide, 72dpi JPEG that you placed there earlier.

3 Now press Ctrl+A to select both images and press the Center button on the formatting bar to centre the images on the page. Deselect both images by clicking the right arrow direction key once and then hit return. The cursor will again move down one line.

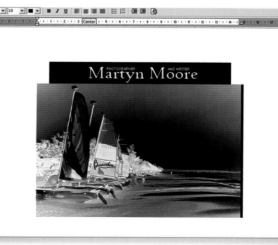

Step by Step building a web page (cont.)

4 We are going to type a simple message about you underneath the photo and then provide an email link that will automatically open an email message for visitors whose web browsers are properly configured with their email programs. Type your message in the font, size and colour you prefer and then type 'Email: you@your. mail' replacing you@your.mail with your own email address. Highlight your email address and then click on the hyperlink icon, the one with the small globe and chain on it. In the Insert Hyperlink box, click on 'An email address'. This will start the text box with the Mailto: command. Click inside the text box immediately after Mailto: and type this: you@your. mail?subject=A message from the website. Then click OK.

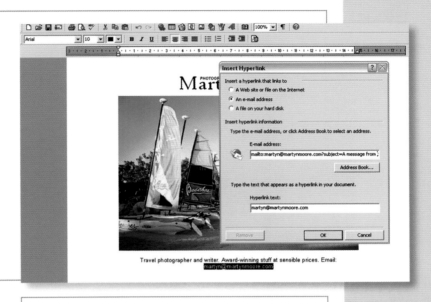

Travel photographer and writer. Award-winning stuff at sensible prices. Email: martyn@martynmoore.com

5 Your email address is now blue and underlined. If you click on it, it will open up an email message with your email address already on it and 'A message from the website' already typed into the message's subject line. This allows you to identify which emails have come to you from your website and so monitor response.

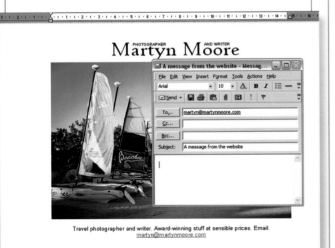

Travel photographer and writer. Award-winning stuff at sensible prices. Email: martyn@martynmoore.com

6 You have now almost finished your first web page. All you have to do now is save it in the right format, as an HTML page (.htm or .html), in your folder called Publish. From the File menu, go to Save As… and choose HTML Document. Call the file 'index'. It's important to call this first page index because when a web browser goes to a site, it always opens the file called index first. Click OK. Now the dialog box will warn you that some formatting will be lost if you save 'index' as an HTML file. Click OK. We can use the lost formatting to learn about editing code.

Travel photographer and writer. Award-winning stuff at sensible prices. Email: martyn@martynmoore.com

Editing code

If you look in the Publish folder now, you will see a web page file called 'index' and two numbered image files. When the word processor saves a page as a web page, it also saves new copies of the images into the same folder from where you create the web page. These new image files are the ones that the page is linked to, so these are the ones that must be uploaded to the web server when you publish the site. Proper web page editors don't create copies of the images; they refer to the images in the appropriate folders that you created when you organized your images.

If you double-click on the index file, it will open up in your web browser software – Internet Explorer or something similar. Now you can see where the formatting was lost when you saved the file: the text and email link under the photo are no longer centred, they have moved to the left. This is another peculiarity of using a word processor instead of a web editor, but we are going to use it to our advantage.

Many web builders who write HTML code do so in a simple text editor. This is a highly skilled operation requiring knowledge of HTML code and programming scripts, but you're not reading this book to learn how to do that. However, a little adjustment to the code of the page you have just created will be good for your soul.

1 With the index page open in Internet Explorer, go to the View menu and choose Source. This will open up a text window; if you are on a PC, then it will use the Notepad program. In this window you can see the HTML code that creates that page you just built. It will look strange and complex, but if you study it for a few minutes, certain parts will start to make sense. For example, you will see the text that you keyed in under the photo and you will see size and position information for the photo and your logo.

2 Look at the detail of the code and compare it to the actual web page displayed. The code is split into two distinct sections: the head, between <HEAD> and </HEAD>, and the body, between <BODY> and </BODY>. The layout information for this page is all in the body section of the code. In front of the references to the images you can see the code <P ALIGN="CENTER"> to keep the images in the centre of the page. But in front of the text you typed you can see just <P>. Use the cursor to highlight the code <P ALIGN="CENTER"> and use Ctrl+C to copy it. Now use the cursor to highlight the <P> right in front of the text and use Ctrl+V to paste <P ALIGN="CENTER"> in place of <P>.

3 From the File menu of Notepad choose Save and then close down this text window. Now press the Refresh button of Internet Explorer and, with a bit of luck, you should find when the window reloads that the text on the document index has now been centred.

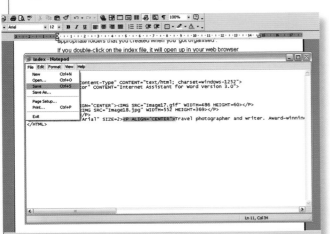

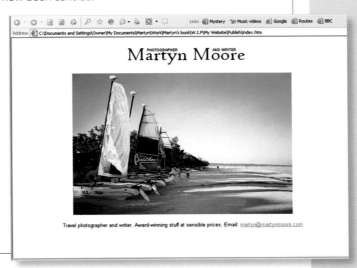

4 You can learn a lot about HTML code simply by changing values in the Notepad view of the code, saving the file and then looking at the results in the browser. You can easily edit the displayed text from inside the code, but try changing the font size (shown as <FONT FACE="Arial" SIZE=2>) and see what happens. Look at the effect on the way the image is displayed when you change either the WIDTH or HEIGHT values. You probably won't want to save this change because the original settings are correct for the actual size of the images. But you can see how the images can be distorted and the quality affected by not displaying them at the optimum size. Finally, when you are satisfied that the page looks okay on your own machine, you can publish it to the web. If you are hosting your pages on a free community site like Tripod, there will be an upload section that allows you to publish files to your web space via the browser window. Simply use that page to upload the page file called 'index' and the two numbered image files from within your Publish folder.

7

Using an FTP program

Now let's look at the slightly harder way of uploading a web page. Earlier, we mentioned FTP programs (see page 33), and you probably downloaded one from the website at www.websitesforphotographers.co.uk. Now you're going to get a chance to use it.

By now, you will have decided what type of hosting you need. You will have chosen either the hosting provided by your Internet service provider or a free community web service that places adverts on your site. Alternatively, you may have chosen to buy hosting from one of the places that registered your domain name for you.

Somewhere on your hosting services website you will be able to find instructions for uploading files to your web space via file transfer protocol, or FTP. There will be a name of a server, starting ftp. You will also need a password, which might be the same password that you use to log on to the Internet. This is how you use FTP to upload pages to your site.

Step by Step using an FTP program

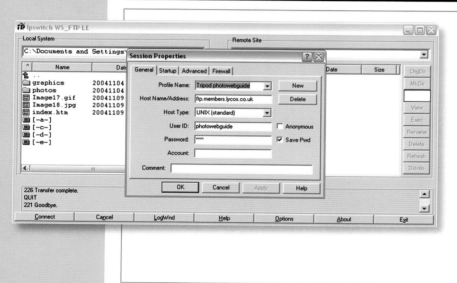

1 A standalone FTP program will have to be downloaded and installed on your machine. Ipswitch WS_FTP LE is available, among others, via www.websitesforphotographers.co.uk. Try one or two and see which you like the best. Open up the FTP program and work out how to set up an account using the username and password information provided to you by the hosting company. When prompted, enter the information provided by your web host (this can usually be saved, so you will only have to do this once) and click 'connect'. With a bit of luck you will now see a window that shows your empty web space. It might already have an index page in there – a holding page created for you by the host when you reserved that space. You can delete that.

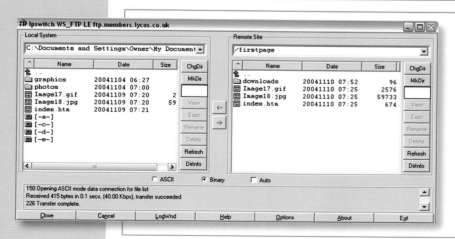

2 Another window, usually to the left, will be looking at your local computer. Use the navigation menus and icons to show the contents of your Publish folder in this window. You should be able to see your new index file and the two numbered image files. Highlight these three files and click the arrow button that sends them to the other window. Some FTP programs allow you to drag and drop the files. In this example, the graphics and photos folders have not been transferred because the word processor made its own copies of the images. These are uploaded instead.

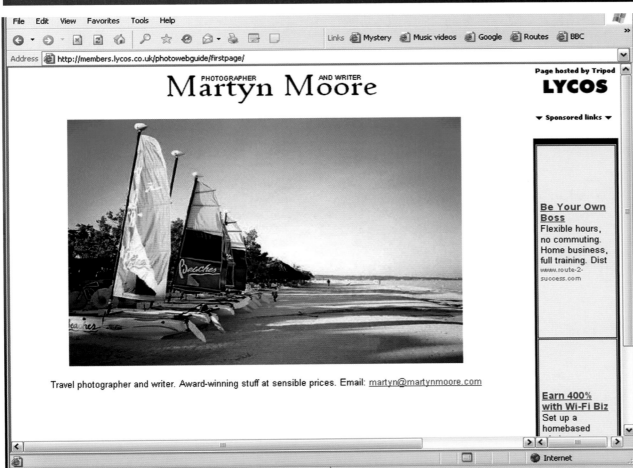

3 If you created your first page in a proper web design program, it won't have created the numbered copies of the images, but linked to the images you saved to the folders called Graphics and Photos. In this case, you should upload the index file and the two folders as well. The contents of the left, local, window must exactly match the right, remote server window for all your links and images to work properly. As you progress to more ambitious multi-page websites, it will be this discipline that causes you most trouble. Go back to Chapter 5 to make sure you are organizing your materials properly (see pages 62–65).

4 The last thing you might have to do is make sure that any domain names you registered now point at the page you have just created. Different hosts, name brokers and administrators have different procedures for doing this, so you will just have to go with the instructions you have been given.

You have now created a web page using a word processor. You have also edited the HTML code of that page using a text editor. You have uploaded the page and two associated images to your web space via FTP and you have pointed your domain name to it. Well done! Congratulate yourself.

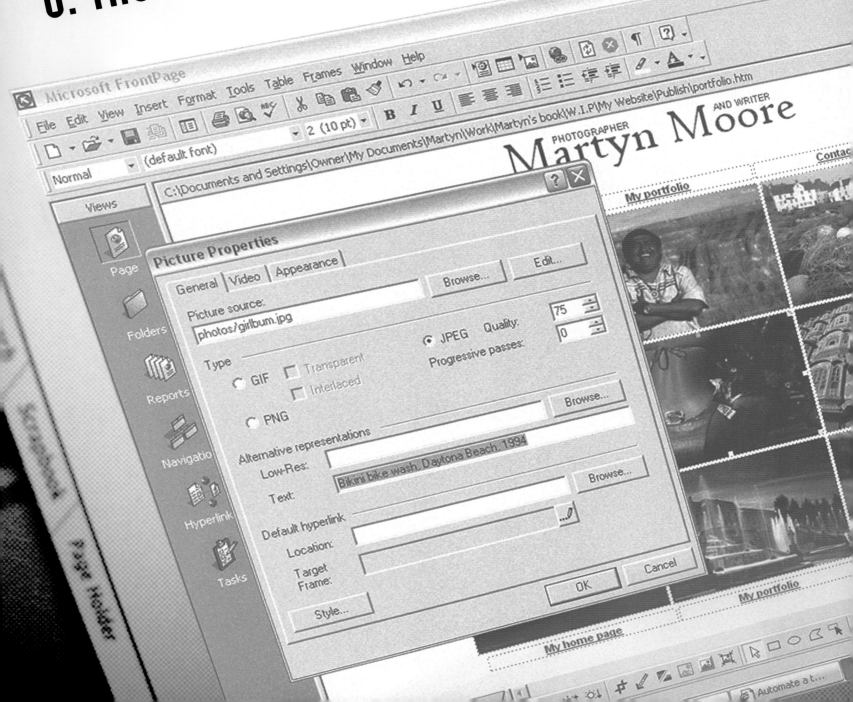

8:

The benefits of a three-page site

You can do a lot with a one-page website, but why stop there? Constructing a three-page website expands your business and creative opportunities and does not require you to have significantly more advanced web-building skills. The three-page website consists of the index page or homepage, the contact page and the portfolio page. Building a three-page website involves thinking about navigation and how to move your visitors logically through the site. All this is explained in this chapter.

8 | Creating a three-page site

■ **If you have stuck with this book up till now, you will have created the simplest type of website – a single page with your logo, a photo, a short message about yourself, and a way for people to get in touch with you. Assuming that you have enjoyed yourself and have experienced a gratifying sense of achievement, you won't want to stop there. A single web page can do a lot and look good, but a three-page site, consisting of an index page, a contact page, and a portfolio page, can look a lot better. Here's how you can build one.**

Creating the index page

Coping with the idiosyncrasies of building a three-page website with a word processor will very probably drive you insane. A more healthy alternative would be to visit the Downloads section of the website, www.websitesforphotographers.co.uk, and get yourself a copy of the useful program Nvu.

Alternatively, you could use Microsoft FrontPage, Macromedia Dreamweaver or another proper web design program. The pictures that are used in this book feature FrontPage 2000. It's simple, it's smart and a more recent version is now available as part of the Office suite of programs.

The first step of building a three-page website is to create a new version of the homepage. This page will be very similar to the one that we previously made in the word processing program. However, because we are now working with a proper web design program, the page will continue to link to the images in their respective folders, rather than create copies. At this stage, you can delete the old index file and the numbered image files in your Publish folder, or you can create another folder for old versions of your site in My Website and move them into that.

Step by Step creating the index page

1 Re-create your index page in the web design program by opening a new page and immediately saving it in the Publish folder as 'index'. It's important to do this before you start inserting pictures or links because this action establishes the new page in the Publish folder and makes sure all images and links are created relative to that page location. Insert your logo and main photo on the blank page. Add the text and email link, just as you did in the word processor and save your work. You should now be at the stage you reached using the word processor, but with the inserted images still in their respective folders and correctly linked.

2 Save yourself time by creating two new pages based on the design of the first. With the index page open, go to the File menu and choose Save As… Now save a second version of this page in the same folder (Publish) and call it 'portfolio'. Now choose Save As… again and call a third version 'contact'. So your publish folder now has three identical pages, each with a different name. Close 'contact' and re-open 'index'. This is important.

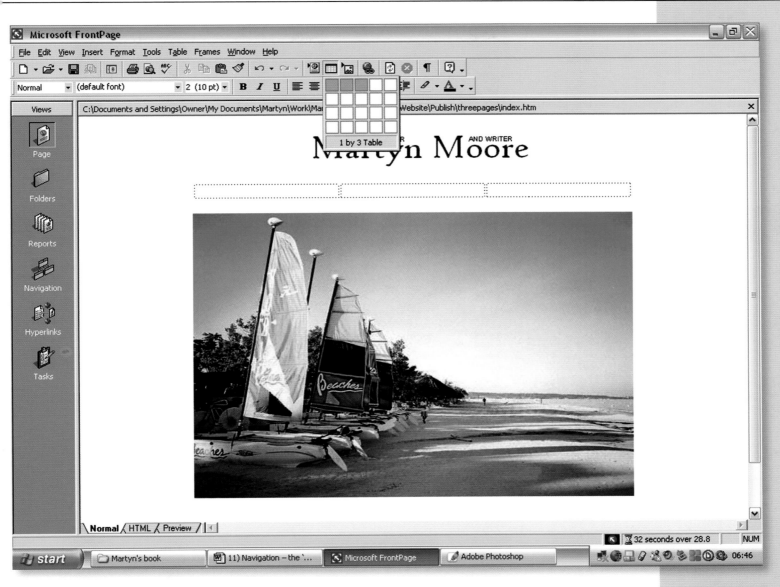

Navigation

Because we are creating a three-page website, we now have to consider the additional element of navigation – the business of a visitor moving between the pages and finding their way around your website. The navigation of this new site is going to be built around a simple 'table' concept.

We didn't use tables in the last chapter, but they are very simple. Tables appear in word processors too, and are used when you want to arrange information in a grid of rows and columns. The table can be placed on a web page and its size and position defined.

Within each of the table's 'cells' we can place text or images and our web editor will allow us to make changes such as the appearance of text, the space between the cells and define each cell's border. The text or images in the cells can be turned into hyperlinks and clicked to go to a new page. Tables are a very useful web design device.

We're creating with FrontPage now – a proper web editor. Here a table has been created, three cells wide and one cell deep, to incorporate a horizontal navigation bar between the logo and the main image. Links to other pages will be created in the table cells.

1 Place the cursor at the right-hand end of your logo graphic and hit Return to create a new line between the two images. Using the Table button on the toolbar or by selecting Table from the Insert menu, create a table three cells across by one cell deep – a single row of three cells. From the Table menu, choose Properties and then Table and change the alignment to Centered. The three cells should now sit above the main photo and below your logo. In the left-hand cell, type 'My homepage'. In the centre cell, type 'My portfolio'. In the right-hand cell, type 'Contact me'. Format the text, choosing your preferred typeface and size. Really, you should limit your use of fonts to the ones described on pages 51–52. You can also play around with the table and cell properties to make each cell the same size and centre the text in them. Properties can be used to change the space between the cells and how you want the borders to appear, if at all.

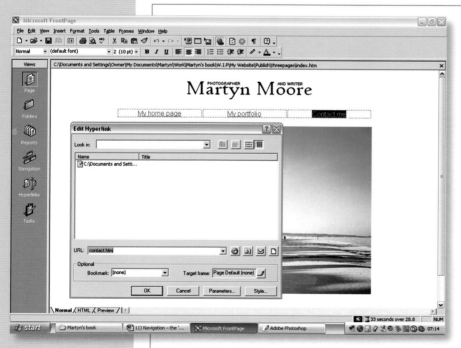

2 When you are happy with the appearance of the table, you can highlight the text in each cell, one at a time, and create the hyperlinks to the other pages using the hyperlink button or command in your web page editing program. Most allow you to click through to the page you want to link, or type its name in a text box.

Organization of files and having pages in the right location when linking them is as important as when you insert images. If the links point to the wrong place, the site won't work.

The most common mistake is to include the local machine information in the link. Then, when you put the page on the web server the link tries to find a file on the machine on your desk. Watch out for that one.

3 Link 'My portfolio' to the page you created called 'portfolio', link the words 'Contact me' to the page called 'contact', and even though this is the index page, you should also link 'My homepage' to the page called 'index'.

In effect, what you have created here is the main navigation bar. It has the names of the three areas of the site we will create and each of those area names has been linked to a page that will feature that content. This entire table can be highlighted, copied (using Ctrl+C or Apple+C), and then pasted (Ctrl+V/Apple+V) anywhere on the website. So start by copying it and then pasting a second version below the main photo and use Table Properties to centre it again.

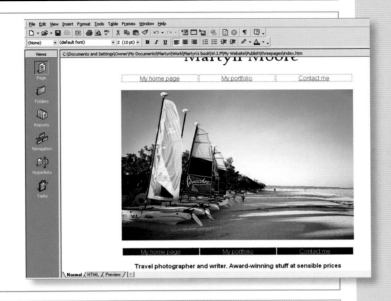

4 This shows a hyperlink being created from the logo at the top of the page and this link goes to the 'index' or homepage. It is an unwritten rule of web design that the logo at the top of the page is linked to the homepage, so all the logos throughout the site should do this. Highlight your GIF file and create the link to the file 'index'. It doesn't matter that this is the index page and that you are linking the page to itself. All will become clear later when you use this page as a template for others and choose Save As... You will also see that the main image has been replaced by a new one from the Photos folder in Publish. This is to differentiate it from the one-page site built earlier. Both these sites can be seen live via www. websitesforphotographers.co.uk.

5 Highlight your main photo and create a hyperlink to the page you called 'portfolio'. This will allow a visitor to see other photographs by clicking on the main one on your homepage. Spend some time in Page Properties, under the Format menu, and decide on the colours for your hyperlinks. You can also set all the hyperlinks to open the new pages in the same window. This should be the default setting for links to pages in your own site. We will open pages from external sites in a new window when we create the 'contact' page.

By now your main navigation is created and the page called 'index' is now linked up to both of the other pages. It even creates links back to itself. This might seem a bit pointless, but it is about to become very useful.

Creating the contact page

The next step then is to create the second page – the contact page.

1 When you are happy with all the navigation on 'index', go to the Save As… command again in the File menu and re-save the whole page as 'portfolio' (we'll discuss this third page later). You will get a warning that this page already exists, but ignore this and overwrite it. Now choose Save As… again and this time call it 'contact', overwriting your existing contact page.

You have just saved yourself a lot of time because what you have created is a set of identical pages, all linked each to the other, but all with different names. Now you can go into each page in turn and edit it while leaving all the basic navigation elements in place.

The contact page is the one that's open already, so let's work on that one first.

2 Highlight the main photo image by clicking on it and then press delete. In its place you can now create your contact information text.

You can include your real-world address, phone and fax details, and an email link similar to the one we created on the single-page site in the last chapter (see pages 78–87).

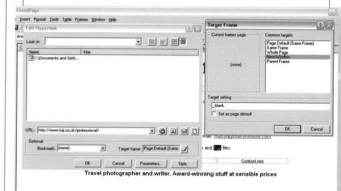

3 But you don't have to stop there. As you can see from the illustration, there is also a short biography together with more pictures. The mugshot is stored in the photos folder in Publish, the signature lives in graphics, and they both add a friendly, personal touch.

This page might also be a good place to add links to the sites of people or organizations that have helped you over the years.

When you set up these hyperlinks, it is important to have the external sites open up in a new window, rather than replace your site in the same window. Your site will stay open under the new site in the new window, allowing visitors to return easily to your pages.

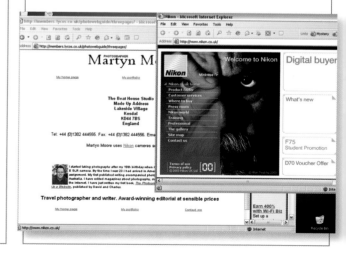

Creating the portfolio page

Finally, there is the portfolio page. By visiting this part of your site, visitors are going to see nine of your favourite photographs; nine pictures that you think demonstrate your talent as a photographer.

Step by Step creating the portfolio page

1 First choose these nine landscape-format digital pictures and put unedited versions into the Raw Images folder of My Website. Now you know why you chose to get CDs with your prints for the last couple of years.

2 The first image we created for the single-page site was 600 pixels wide, so assuming it was a traditional photographic size, the aspect ratio (width to height) will be about 400 pixels deep. We would like to fit the nine pictures into a similar area to that occupied by the main front-page image. Therefore, using your image editor, create new versions of the nine photographs at a resolution of 72dpi and make them 200 pixels wide by 133 pixels deep. You might have to crop photos that don't fit the photographic aspect ratio exactly. Don't just change one of the dimensions, as this will distort the image.

3 Save all nine photos in the photos folder inside Publish and give them short, recognizable names.

4 Now open the portfolio page, highlight the main image and delete it. In the same way as we put the navigation links into a table, we're now going to arrange the nine photos in a table.

Create a table that has three rows and three columns – nine cells in all – and, under Table Properties, centre it on the page. Click in the top right cell and then, using the Insert Picture technique you learned earlier, place the first of your nine pictures from your photos folder in this cell. If you're working with Nvu and are asked for some text at this stage, read ahead to Step 6.

5 Now click on the second cell along and insert the next picture. Repeat this until all the pictures have each been placed in a cell.

In Microsoft FrontPage, the cell sizes adjust to the size of the photographs. You might have to adjust the cell or table properties in other programs to make it look right. For this exercise we used landscape-format images, but no doubt you will have lots of portrait-format pictures in your collection too, and maybe some square ones. There's nothing to stop you placing these images into cells, but you won't achieve the same formal arrangement. Making a block of images the same size and shape as the main image on your homepage will take a bit more working out of picture, table and cell sizes.

Having placed all nine pictures in their table cells, it is unlikely that you will have chosen the perfect order first time. It's worth swapping images around to avoid subject and colour clashes in the arrangement.

You might have noticed, when looking at web pages, that if your cursor rests over an image, a small text box with a pale yellow background pops up.

This text usually provides some information about the image; its main purpose is to provide the viewer with information if, for some reason, the image hasn't loaded in the page. It's known as 'Alternative' text.

6 Let's add some Alternative text to every image on the site. Click on an image in your portfolio table and work out how your design program allows you to edit Image Properties. In FrontPage, you can right-click the image and choose Properties, or select the image and go via the Format menu. Nvu works in exactly the same way and won't even allow you to place an image without Alternative text being entered. Dreamweaver provides an input box for Alternative text in the working area across the bottom of the window.

Work your way through every image on all three pages of your site, adding a line of Alternative text to each. Save each page before closing it and moving along to the next one.

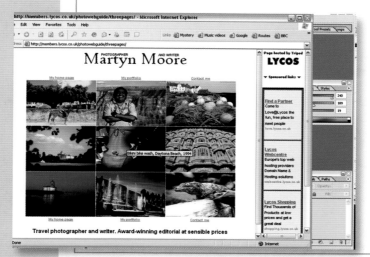

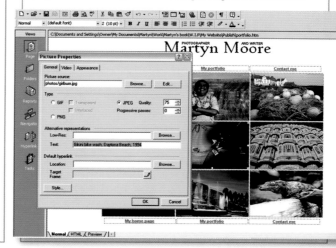

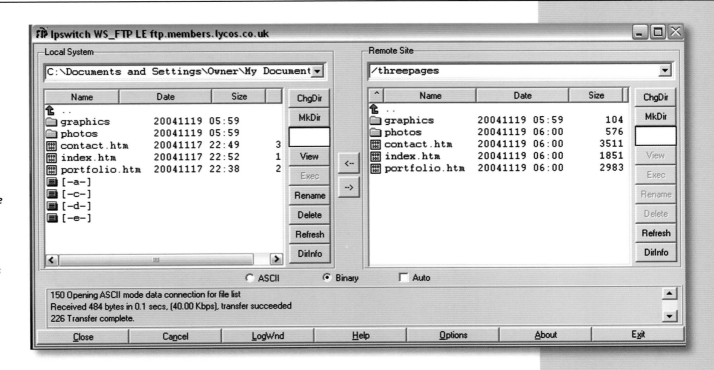

When the time comes to transfer your website files and folders to the web server, FTP (file transfer protocol) software shows you your local hard drive and the remote computer in adjacent windows. If the site works on your machine, replicate the contents on the web server exactly. With WS_FTP, files can be dragged between the windows or highlighted then moved using the arrow buttons.

Fine-tuning and checking

When you have finished the fine-tuning of all your pages, close down your web page editing program and go to the three HTML files that you have previously created in the Publish folder. If you double-click on 'index', this will open up in your web browser and you can then start to test your new website. You should make sure that all the links move you around the site in the way that you expected. If you are connected to the Internet while you do this, you can check any of the links that you have made to external sites and make sure that they open up in a new window.

Remember that all the links to other pages on your own site should open up in the same window. If you find any bugs, gremlins or things that don't work, you will have to go back into the page using the editor and fix it.

At this stage you should also do a very thorough proofread of all the text on the site. Look out for spelling mistakes and bad grammar; try to spot double spaces or other typing errors. You want your site to look as professional as possible.

Uploading the site

Only when the site has been thoroughly checked should you upload it to the web. If you are uploading your new three-page site to the same web space as you did the single-page version, the process will be very similar. The first difference is that there will already be files on the remote server – the original index file and the two numbered pictures created by the word processor. The FTP programs available for download from www.websitesforphotographers.co.uk allow you to replace existing files when you upload a new file with the same name. That's what happens with the 'index' files – the new one simply replaces the old one.

The two numbered image files are now redundant and can be deleted from the web server. They are going to be replaced by the folders you called 'photos' and 'graphics' and all their image file contents.

Ultimately, you need to have exactly replicated the contents of your local Publish folder in the public documents area of your web server. The contents of the local and remote windows should be identical.

Those of you who are accessing the contents of your web server via a web browser window might have to work slightly differently. The web-based FTP access on Tripod, for example, doesn't allow you to upload a folder and its contents. With this system, you have to create a new folder on the web server with exactly the same name as the one in Publish (so, one 'photos' and one 'graphics') and then open each folder (local and remote) and transfer the contents from your machine's folder to the second version on the web server. It's quite simple, so you will only have to read that last bit once more to get the gist of the process.

The curse of caches

So, now you have three pages: 'index', 'contact' and 'portfolio', and two folders of images: 'photos' and 'graphics' published to the web. Close the FTP program, open your web browser and type in your web address… Damn! It's still the old single-page site!

This is the curse of caching. There are millions of files on the Internet and we often look at hundreds of them in a day. In order to speed up our access to sites, copies of them sit on other web servers between the original live site and users. When new versions of sites are published, it can take some time for the latest version to spread out across these 'caches'. High-traffic news sites propagate very, very quickly and sites that call up words and pictures from a database, known as 'dynamic' sites, update almost instantly.

But we're getting ahead of ourselves here. In short, don't be surprised if it takes several hours for your three-page miracle to appear in your browser.

Speaking of your browser, that too has a cache where previously viewed content is stored for faster downloading. You can clear out these files by going to Internet Options under the Tools menu of Internet Explorer, or the Empty Cache option of Safari. Be careful using Favourites, or bookmarks, too. They can lead to you viewing old versions of sites.

When you've tried all this, all there is left to do is sit and keep refreshing your page in the browser window.

The command is under the View menu, or just keep pressing the F5 function key on a PC.

Troubleshooting

At some stage, and it may even be the first time you try, you will see your new web pages in all their glory. And now the whole world can see them too.

It is a safe bet that something won't work and it will probably be a picture, or possibly a link between pages. The problem here is that although you read and re-read these last two chapters, you got something out of whack. Maybe you picked up the wrong version of an image, or inserted it into the page from a different folder. Even if the image found its way into the correct folder for uploading, if it wasn't in that folder when you inserted it, then the page is looking for it in the wrong place.

The vast majority of problems are down to some small oversight involving the Insert action. There are a lot of things to get right. If the correct photo was in the photos folder at the time it was inserted into the portfolio page and saved; and if the photos folder was in the Publish folder and the portfolio page was saved into Publish next to it; and the contents of Publish are exactly mirrored on the web server, then it will work.

But you have to be able to say that about every image and every folder and every link and every page.

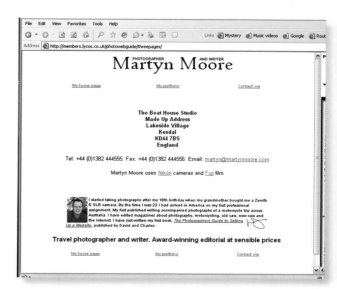

This three-page site was created as this book was written. Clarity and ease of description have defined the content and layout. It may not be the most inspirational site, but it does show what can be done with the most basic resources.

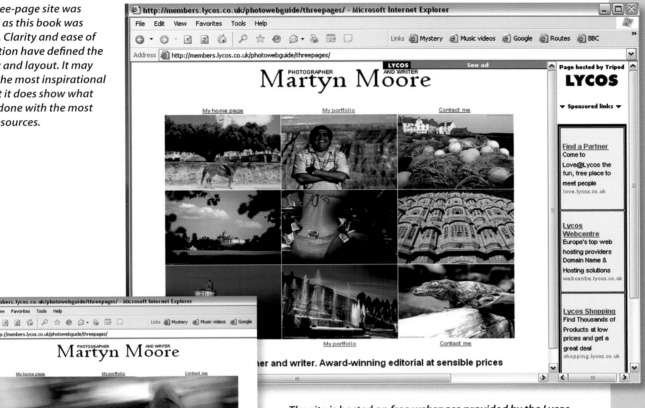

The site is hosted on free webspace provided by the Lycos service Tripod. The company raises revenue by posting advertisements down the right-hand side of the page, and a large-format ad obscures the page when it first loads.

If any item has moved relative to another, or if any name has changed, then errors will result.

This is your first big test. Your resolve to fix these errors will tell you a lot about how much you want to build websites. If you are keen to dive back into the web page editor and the folder and file structure to repair broken links, this indicates that you have a good positive attitude and a penchant for problem-solving.

If you find yourself selecting View and then Source from a browser menu, or choosing 'HTML view' in a

page editor to unravel all the lines of code and spot an irregularity, then you might even have the makings of a geek. Good for you.

If, on the other hand, you went to your homepage and clicked your way around three new pages, saw all the images at the right size and in the right place, and all the links to external websites went where they were supposed to through new windows… then, well done. You have created and uploaded your three-page website with no glitches. The rest of us hate you.

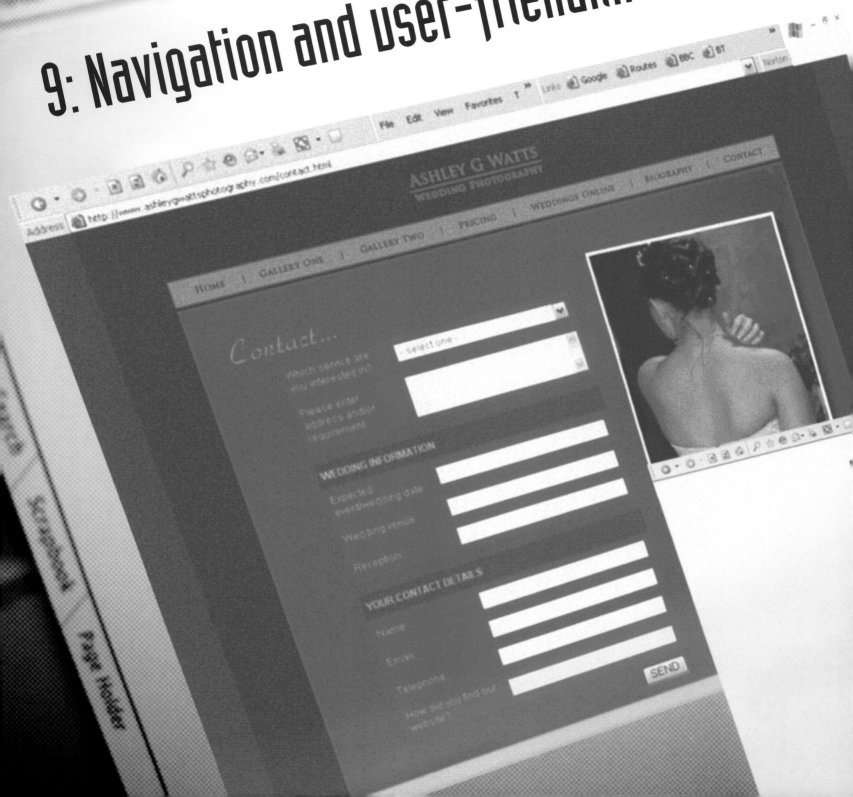

9:

Navigation and user-friendliness

Creating a website entails meeting the expectations of your visitors. The Internet is a relatively young medium, but there are already certain established 'rules' that you should follow to help your site-users navigate around easily. Having a slickly designed, user-friendly website will help to enhance your professional image and may ultimately help you make more sales or gain more contacts. This section looks at valuable tactics such as consistency of design and the Three Click Rule. It also looks at how to handle responses from your visitors.

9 | Meeting users' expectations

Internet users have come to expect certain things from a website, especially when it comes to ease of navigation. There are certain rules that you should follow to make your site easy to move around and user-friendly. After all, once you have brought people to your site, you want them to stay there and, ultimately, you want them to use your services. A user-friendly website is all part of a good business strategy.

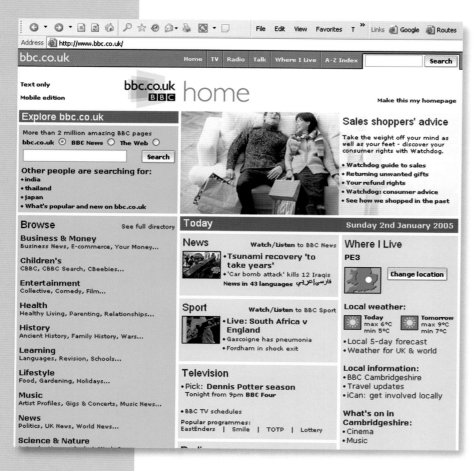

The homepage at www.bbc.co.uk is a jumping-off point for many other site sections, so almost every item on it is clickable: every logo, every image, every heading, sub-heading and list item takes you somewhere if you click on it.

User expectations

We touched on one of the rules of good web design in the last chapter when we made the site's logo on each page click through to the homepage (see page 93). There are a lot of unwritten rules in web design that have become established in the relatively short time that the Internet has been a popular medium, and the convention of the site logo linking to the homepage, usually the one called 'index', is almost universal.

As people use the Internet more and more often, the behaviour of the sites they visit starts to define their expectations. Sites that are designed intuitively are easy to navigate and the common navigation techniques used by web designers become established as rules.

For example, on a news site, the homepage will carry an edited version of a story – a taster. Ninety-nine times out of a hundred, the headline of that taster will click through to the full story. If the taster has a small thumbnail photo with it, then that too will click through to the story, and the story will probably feature a larger version of the photo. But neither the thumbnail photo nor the headline will say 'Click here' on it. People just expect that to be how it works.

Text links to other pages usually change colour after they have been clicked through. This helps visitors to see where they have already been on the site.

Digital Photo magazine doesn't try to do too much with its website. There's a friendly welcome page (right) and a helpful contact page (below), each with clear invitations to subscribe to the print magazine. There is also good cross-promotion with its sister magazine, Practical Photography.

What is clickable and what is not is increasingly defined by convention, but a great rule is: 'If it will help, make it clickable.'

Visitors have also become accustomed to seeing a link change colour when their mouse pointer floats over it. This is achieved by using JavaScript or dynamic HTML – short codes that instruct parts of the page to behave in certain ways. Scripts can be used to pop up new windows automatically and close them down. They can be made to add the page to a visitor's bookmarks or Favourites list and even make the page that they're viewing their homepage – the first page they see when they open up their Internet browser.

Scripts such as these are also behind 'Print this page' commands and 'Email this to a friend' features. We have collected these useful scripts on the website together with full instructions on how to use them on your own web pages. Go and see them for yourself at www.websitesforphotographers.co.uk.

One engaging feature on the Digital Photo site is its humorous 'Daft & Strange' section. Visitors are encouraged to use techniques explained in the magazine to create funny images of the magazine in unusual situations.

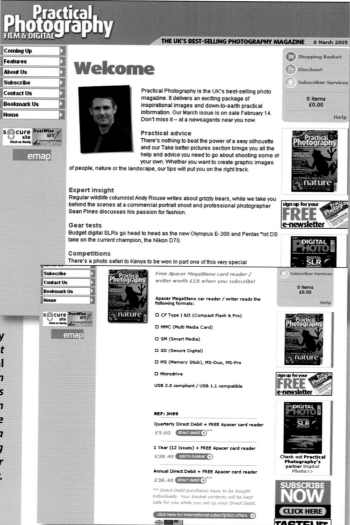

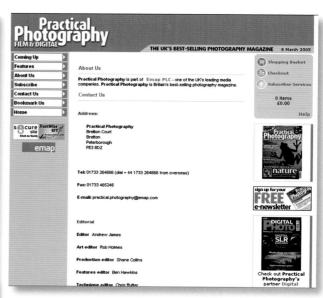

9

Practical Photography returns the compliment and promotes Digital Photo magazine on its site. Again, there is a strong emphasis on subscriptions to the print magazine and a button encouraging visitors to sign up for an e-newsletter.

The e-newsletter sign-up is on every page. These messages to subscribers are part of the brand's online strategy.

Links within a website

There should be many ways of getting from one part of a website to another. Lots of websites have several links to the same place on each page. Remember that magazine publishing company that cropped up in Chapter 2 (see page 23)? Well, the people involved decided that one of the most useful things their magazine websites could do was to sell subscriptions to the magazines online. Consequently, every page had several links to the page where subscription orders were placed. They used button links that flashed the message 'Subscribe

Now!'; they had simple text links that said 'Click here to subscribe'; quasi-news stories explained the benefits of subscribing and featured links from the headline, the image and the last line, which said: 'For more information, click here.' Even the images of the magazine's front cover clicked through to a page promoting subscriptions off the back of the latest issue's contents.

Working out the number of different ways in which people can move around your website is part of the fun of designing the site. Think of it as a challenge to be as user-friendly as possible. You can use horizontal navigation or tabs to click through to sections, you can use vertical columns on the left or right, or you can use both. You can put 'click here' on all the clickable bits, or you can put it on just some of them. It's always best to flag up the links if you want to really help navigation.

Of course, the bigger a site gets, the more pages it has, and the more complex this navigation can become. It is essential to have a clear link back to the homepage on every page in the site. Once you start dividing your website into sections, then a link back to the section homepage might be enough, but you will still be providing the link back to the main index page via the logo, won't you?

The Three Click Rule

A gallery section is a good example to consider here. If you create a series of galleries, then a page listing all the galleries becomes the gallery section homepage. Each individual gallery must link back to this list of galleries, and this list of galleries must link back to the main website homepage. This arrangement obeys what is known as the 'Three Click Rule'.

The Three Click Rule says that no part of your website should be more than three clicks away from any other part of your website. It's a very good rule.

When you drew your first site plan (see pages 56–61), the pages cascaded down from the homepage like a family tree. Each level down introduces the need for an extra level of navigation to take visitors back up. The three-page site we created in Chapter 8 uses only horizontal navigation. Visitors move sideways from one page to another and all pages are linked to each other.

Now imagine that the portfolio page is a list of galleries. Maybe you have a people gallery, a places gallery, and one or two specialist galleries. By clicking on individual galleries, a visitor is 'drilling down' into the gallery section and you have to start thinking about how you will navigate them back up again.

There are many ways to reach the photography content on the BBC website. Typing 'photography' into the search facility will provide dozens of articles, but there are other ways.

If a gallery homepage with clickable thumbnails opens in a new window, then each full-size image can open in that same window. The gallery homepage should have a 'close this window' button and each full-size image page should have a 'back to thumbnails' button. If the gallery homepage opens in the same window as the main site, then it must have all the navigation to help the visitor back into the site. Really user-friendly galleries also allow the viewer to click through all of the full-size images by clicking 'next' and 'previous' buttons.

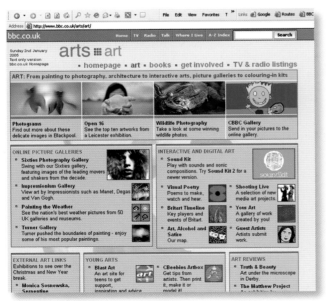

After clicking on Arts, under the Society & Culture heading, the Sixties Photography Gallery appears on the Arts section homepage. The gallery itself is just three clicks from the site homepage and by clicking on the site logo, top left, the homepage is just one click back.

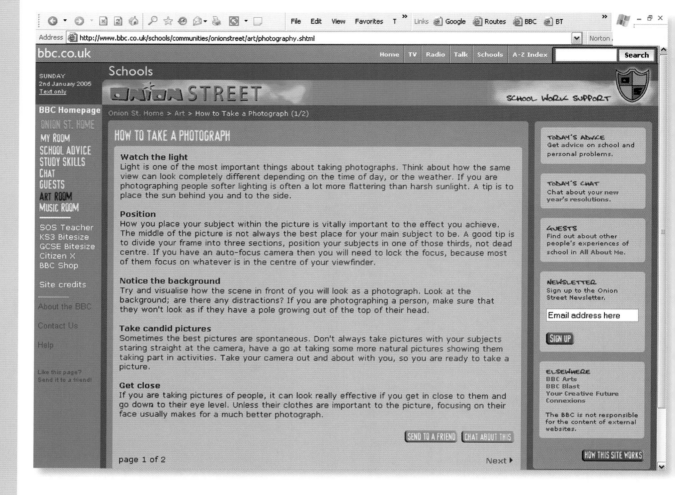

If it's basic instructions you want, or projects and inspiration for children, the BBC has that, too. From the homepage, Onion Street's How To Take a Photograph is just three clicks away from the Schools link.

You should never lead a visitor down a blind alley. Every page you take them to must have clear navigation to show them the way back. If every page links to a section homepage, with every section homepage linking to the site homepage, then you have the Three Click Rule working up out of the site for you too.

Massive websites, like the one from the BBC or Microsoft Networks at www.msn.com, will always strive to obey the Three Click Rule despite their size. It has sections within sections and visitors can drill down to content that seems to be dozens of clicks from the homepage. The way BBC designers, for example, get around this is by treating various sections as websites in their own right. The BBC homepage is like a portal site into the huge world of the BBC, including television, radio, news, sport,

lifestyle and special interests. Nevertheless, it's always easy to get back to the main index and an incredible amount of content is just three clicks away.

Consistency throughout the site

It is vital to maintain consistency throughout the site. We looked at consistency of look and feel in Chapter 4 (see pages 48–53). Stick with the same colours, fonts, layouts and picture sizes throughout your website. By making all the pages behave in a similar way, the consistency helps the visitor move through the site. When we created the three-page site in Chapter 8, we used the 'Save As…' technique. This will help you to create new pages based on existing ones and retain their important characteristics.

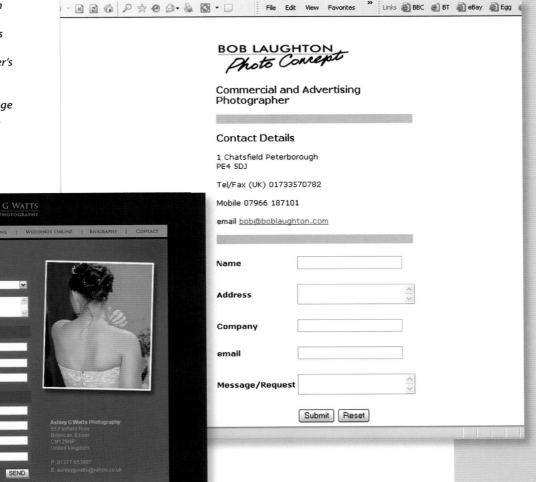

Ashley Watts (below) and Bob Laughton (right) adopt a very similar approach to contact pages. Both provide full address and telephone details, together with a direct email link that works with the user's email program to open a new message. They also provide text boxes to allow visitors to compose messages on the page to be delivered via the site's technology.

We could go wandering off into the world of cascading style sheets here, which is a way of setting up styles that apply to all pages of a website. But that really lies in the realm of the technical manual, and you will learn a lot more from the Dreamweaver or FrontPage user guide if that is something you are interested in.

Contact information

That just about covers the simpler rules of navigation. But there are some other rules to be aware of. Contact information is one of the ways visitors judge how much they can trust a website. Unscrupulous websites, selling dubious products and services or making unsubstantiated claims, often bury any real-world contact information such as an office street address, a permanent, fixed telephone number or the name of a real person – that's if they show them at all.

If you intend to offer a high level of customer care and want the world to think that you are a reliable service provider, then clear contact details are essential. Allowing customers to contact you personally by phone and post as well as by email will make them feel confident about working with you. Of course, for some of you, encouraging this type of communication is at the heart of your website's purpose.

You may feel uncomfortable about publishing details of your home address on an Internet site, especially if

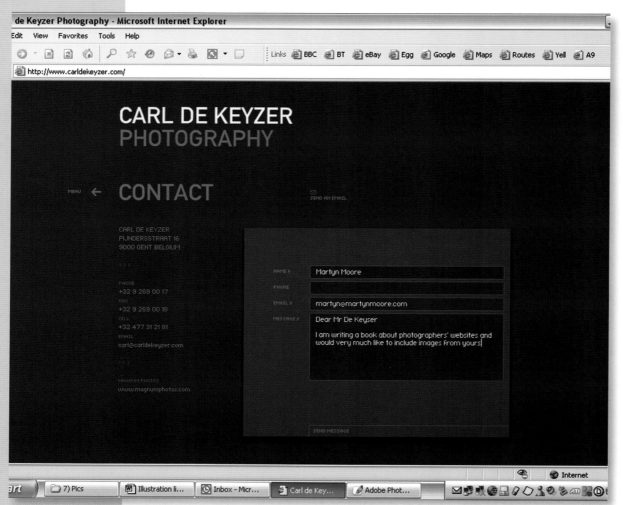

Carl De Keyzer, after amazing us with cutting-edge presentation technology on his homepage and galleries (see page 49), provides a clear, informative contact page with every means of communication catered for.

that same website mentions all the fabulously expensive photographic equipment that you have available for use on an assignment. It's true that this kind of promotion might attract all the wrong kinds of interest. For this reason, it is totally acceptable to set up a post office box number if you would prefer not to invite potential thieves to your home.

Handling responses

Finally, there is the question of handling responses. As the world seems to spin faster and faster every day, people are expecting ever-shorter response times. Back in the days when people wrote lots of letters to each other, you might draft or dictate a letter that would be typed up that day and then placed into an 'out' tray and then the post. The mail service would take two or three days to carry the letter across town, where it would be delivered and read. The response might be prepared within a couple of days and the process would work in reverse.

Today, we may find ourselves firing off hastily written, badly punctuated emails to individuals in some vast corporate multinational based on the other side of the world and if we haven't had a reply by lunchtime, we find ourselves wondering: 'What's the matter with these people? What are they doing? I sent that email twenty minutes ago!' Written communications can receive a response almost as quickly as a telephone call, but why

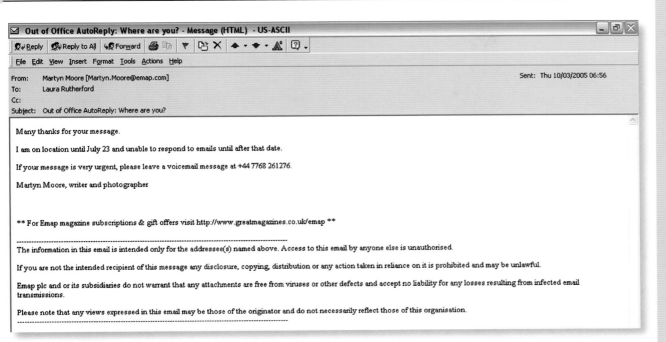

Microsoft Outlook can be used to send an automatic reply when you are unable to respond quickly to emails. This facility is usually available on web-based email access and webmail accounts such as Mail.com. Because email redirects can be set up to forward mail to web-based accounts, you can still keep an eye on incoming messages and provide good customer service while you are away from base.

should they? In the old days, you might have had only one mail delivery or one letter-writing session per day, so written replies took longer and customers accepted this as a matter of fact.

But with email we all, perhaps unreasonably, expect an almost immediate response. So with this in mind, it is important to check your email messages regularly, and reply to them as quickly as possible. If your email system is web-based and you can check it from anywhere in the world, then you can even handle messages when you are on assignment. A quick message back saying: 'Hi customer, thank you for your note. I'm shooting a civil war in Africa today, but will deal with your inquiry when I'm back in the office on Tuesday the 20th.' And, of course, an email system can be set up to fire out this message to everybody who mails you during your trip. Then all you have to do is make it safely back to the office by the 20th.

To start with, handling response from your website will be easy – too easy perhaps, if you are not getting very much. But if it all goes swimmingly, and response picks up, you need to be ready for it. So in the next chapter, we look at managing growth.

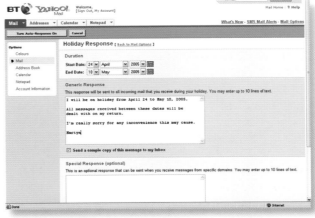

10: Managing the growth of your website

10:

Managing the growth of your website

Having a website can be an excellent business strategy. You need to know how to manage the growth of your business, however, or you could end up being the victim of your own success. If you are a photographer, you need to ensure that you still have time actually to take pictures, rather than just administering to your online clients. At a certain stage, you might need to get more people involved, including a professional web developer. You might even evolve into a professional web developer yourself.

There are many ways in which you can promote your website and, hopefully, start collecting orders from your online visitors. Rapid growth however, might present you with a fresh set of problems, the solutions to which are considered below.

The level of response

It is possible that your website might only provide a perfect level of response for a very short time. There is every chance that you will experience a very long period when you receive little or no response at all. The aim of this section is to make that period as short as possible.

If these ideas work, then you will reach a stage where your site is busy but manageable. It is difficult to predict how long this phase will last – it might just tick along nicely forever.

You could be forgiven for thinking that huge levels of traffic to your website would be a good problem to have, but it might start to make unreasonable demands on your time and even start to cost you a lot of money. Growth needs to be managed.

Advertising in print

The first offline thing you can do to promote your website is to make sure that your web address is included in every item of printed matter that you create. Obviously, business cards need to show your web and email addresses, but so do letters and invoices. Make your web presence a part of your 'with compliments' slips. If you use a stamp for your slide mounts and the backs of prints, have a new one made up with your online details.

If you advertise, then including your website address increases the power of your advertising enormously. Some companies use printed adverts simply to promote their websites, believing that once a potential customer makes it as far as the website then that will do all the selling for them. You can say a lot more online than you

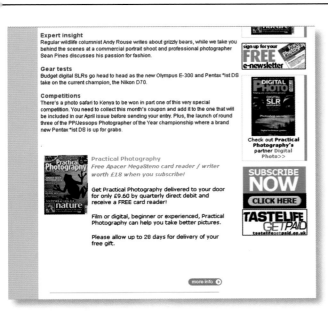

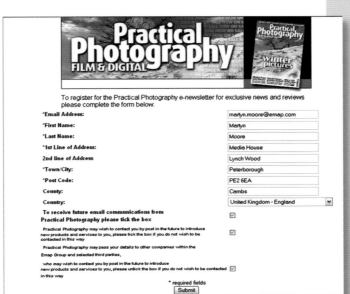

can in a quarter-page magazine advert, so use the advert to get clients to visit you online.

Advertising via email

Email everyone in your contacts list announcing your new website. You now have the skills and resources to send them an HTML email that can look very similar to your site. Creating a graphically rich message with hyperlinks to your site and its sections is easy with Microsoft Outlook. If you go to your own homepage, you can select 'Send' from the 'File' menu of Internet Explorer and email your homepage direct to all your friends and business associates, text, images, links and all.

In fact, you might just create HTML emails instead of a website. Create the message in Outlook itself or put a page together in your web editor and then import it into Outlook. If you save it as a template, then every week you can create a new message to send out. If this message is designed to include your news and contact information, it will do the job of a website. You can dedicate each one to a different subject: an addition to your portfolio or a new service you offer.

HTML emails can link to web pages, so you can use them in conjunction with web content. One web page you really ought to build as part of a message-based online strategy is a single homepage inviting visitors to sign up to receive the messages. There is a form that can be included in the page so that when a visitor adds their details the information is written into a text file that lives on your web server with your pages. The success of an email campaign to attract customers is based entirely on your ability to grow and manage a list of email addresses.

There are legal implications with collecting individuals' data. It must be kept private at all times and you need to be familiar with data protection legislation. Every email you send out should have a link that allows people to unsubscribe if they want to stop getting your messages.

To start with, you will probably send the messages out yourself. Enter all the recipient email addresses into the 'Bcc' box of the message if you don't want them all to be able to see each other. Be aware though, that this makes your message look like 'spam' – or unsolicited junk email – to lots of people's filtering systems. Also, your own, free email account might refuse to send the message to a large number of recipients because it sees your activities as spamming. A paid-for email service might allow you to bulk mail, but as your list grows you might have to start looking for a third-party mailing service to send your HTML messages for you. There are plenty of them around and they will charge you according to the size of your mailing list and the file size of the message.

The Practical Photography website doesn't seem very big for a market-leading magazine brand. The emphasis is on selling print version subscriptions and gathering email addresses from visitors who wish to receive an e-newsletter. When that e-newsletter (far left) arrives, you understand why the site is basic. The e-newsletter is huge, with details of the latest issue of the magazine, features, equipment information, competitions and more. The strategy of delivering relevant information direct to subscribers' inboxes is considerably more effective than having a high-maintenance website.

Advertising via search engines

Telling all the people you are already in contact with is relatively easy. The power of the web lies in reaching those people who have not yet discovered your talents.

The obvious places to go first are the search engines. Back in the old days, you could go to a search engine like Yahoo! and submit a detailed description of your site. Within a few weeks the site would be included in the directory (yes, checked and verified by real people) and what you wrote would probably be your listing. These days, most search engines' listings are generated automatically. Their computers trawl the web indexing sites 24 hours a day, 365 or more days a year.

Left to its own devices, a robot search engine will find your site and list it for free. Unfortunately, typing the word 'photographer' followed by the name of your town might still leave you way down the list of results.

There are a couple of tricks that you can use to improve your results, though. First of all, make sure your name is in the actual name of the page, together with the word photographer and the town where you are based. The title of the page is picked up by search engines, so calling your homepage ('index') something like: 'Angus McOatup, pet photographer, Arbroath' will increase your search engine rankings among photographers who are based in Arbroath.

Another way to improve search engine results is to add 'keywords' to the code in your web pages. To do this, you need to access the source code of your web pages and edit it. Looking at the source code of your web page, either in HTML view of your editing program, or by opening the HTML document in a basic text editor like Notepad, you can see the code is divided into the 'head' section (between <head> and </head>) and the 'body' section (between <body> and </body>). The keywords and description that are picked up by many search engine robots are placed in the head section of code as 'metatags'; instructions for how to create them appear opposite. You can also look at other websites' metatags using the View Source facility on your web browser.

All the big search engines have an area where you can enter details of your website and hopefully see your site appear higher up in its rankings. Most of them offer a free service and a variety of paid-for options. It's worth investigating the price of paid-for performance. The cost is proportional to the number of times a word is searched for.

Step by Step · creating meta tags

1 Open a page on your hard disk in your editing program and go to the HTML view. You can also open this local file in Internet Explorer and then under the 'View' menu choose 'Source'. The text file that displays the HTML code of the page can be edited and saved as the new code for the page.

2 Near the top of the code you can see the 'head' section of the page. It's all the code between the tags <head> and </head>. If you have given this page a title in your web page editor, this will appear in code with the line: <title>Your page name</title>.
On a new line under the title code but within the 'head' section, type:
<meta name="description" content="yourname,photographer,yourtown">

3 Then, on another line, still within the 'head', type:
<meta name="keywords" content="photographer, yourname,yourtown,subjects,cameras">
Change the words yourname, yourtown and subjects to your own personal information. Be careful not to change any other code on the page, save the changes and upload this new version of the file to your website.

```
<!DOCTYPE HTML PUBLIC "-//W3C//DTD HTML 4.01 Transitional//EN">
<html>
<head>
<title>Ronnie Israel, photographer, River Thames</title>
<!-- website & corporate identity designed by Lynda Elliott of InWeb Designs (UK) -->
<meta http-equiv="Content-Type" content="text/html; charset=iso-8859-1">
<meta name="description" content="Our extensive photographic image bank spans over
15 years of development along the River Thames and Docklands.">
<meta name="keywords" content="Ronnie Israel, stock photography, London, United
Kingdom, image bank, Docklands, images, photography, photos, River Thames.">
<META NAME="Subject" CONTENT="Ronnie Israel, professional environmental photographer.">
<META NAME="OWNER" CONTENT="ronnie@ronnieisrael.com">
<META NAME="AUTHOR" CONTENT="Ronnie Israel">
<META HTTP-EQUIV="CONTENT-LANGUAGE" CONTENT="English">
<META HTTP-EQUIV="VW96.OBJECTTYPE" CONTENT="Document">
<META NAME="RATING" CONTENT="General">
<META name="robots" CONTENT="index, follow, all">
<META NAME="Revisit-after" CONTENT="30">
<META http-equiv="Pragma" content="no-cache">
<link rel="stylesheet" href="textr.css" type="text/css">
</head>
```

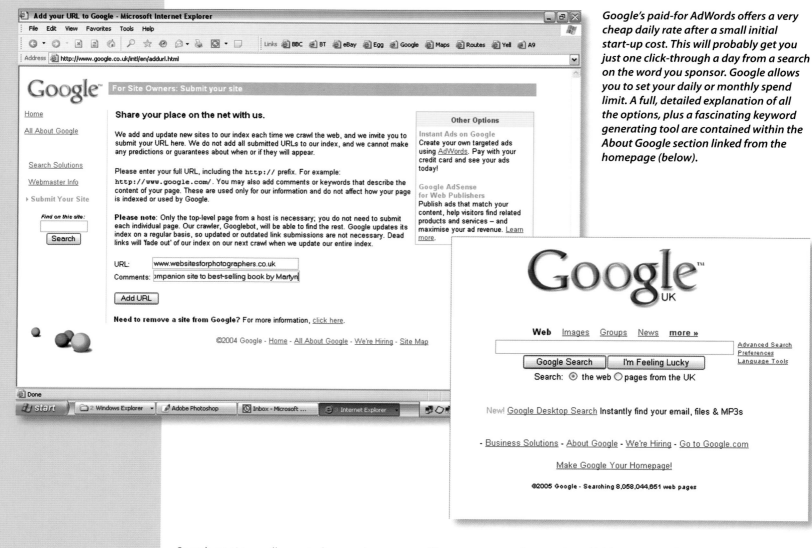

Google's paid-for AdWords offers a very cheap daily rate after a small initial start-up cost. This will probably get you just one click-through a day from a search on the word you sponsor. Google allows you to set your daily or monthly spend limit. A full, detailed explanation of all the options, plus a fascinating keyword generating tool are contained within the About Google section linked from the homepage (below).

Search engines will now index much more specific information about your site based on these keywords. Their robots also pick up all the text on a page, so mentions of your name, what you do and where you are will all register. Another clever trick is to add these words to an image-only page, but below the image, and then make the words the same colour as the page background. Now the search engines will pick them up but viewers of the page won't be able to see them. Sneaky, eh?

With your meta tags in place, the next best thing you can do is take a few hours out to alert a few search engines. Every major search engine has a section where visitors can submit a site for indexing. Follow links to

sections such as: 'Add a site' or 'Submit URL' and key in your details. There are direct links to these sections at the big search engines on the website that accompanies this book: www.websitesforphotographers.co.uk.

One way you can save yourself a bit of time and effort is to create a text file with all the statements about you and your site pre-typed. Have a single line for the site name, another for the homepage address, type out the description in thirty words as one block of text and then add another final line for your email address. As you encounter each submission form, all your text is available for straight copy (Ctrl+C) and paste (Ctrl+V). And all the listings will be consistent.

Local sites from North Wales to Las Vegas will list your business or your event, sometimes for free. Getting involved in the community will result in publicity for your activities on community websites.

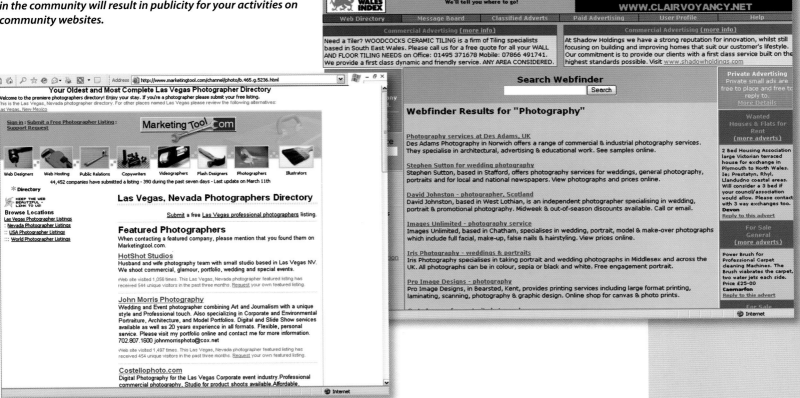

Advertising via a directory

Most people, when they are looking for a photographer to hire, will start off searching locally. Look on the Internet for business directories close to home. Every decent-sized town has a listing site for local businesses and many offer a free directory entry. Spend time submitting your details to every one you can find. A word of warning here: many websites appear to offer free listings and then take you through a lengthy form-filling process, only to reveal their charges at the bottom of the page or just as you submit your details.

If you are going to pay out money for a directory listing, you should make sure you know what you're getting. Wouldn't it be great if somebody launched a huge directory that was free to start with, but we all agreed to pay a nominal fee from the money we earned

from the first commission that site generated? There don't seem to be any about at the moment.

You need to know how much traffic a site gets, what type of searches are most often conducted and how it promotes itself. A directory promotes itself to promote you, so try to avoid paying money to appear on a site that nobody uses.

Local directory sites are still competing with the national ones, which operate at a regional level. If you pay to be listed with a national directory, you will be signing up to a countrywide service that is most often used at a local level. The whole market of online business directories is in a state of flux, with new arrivals arriving on the scene all the time. It is really hard to advise you which one to go for, and at a local level, of course, it's pretty well impossible. Register your details with all the free ones and if you pay, good luck.

Advertising via photography directories

Once you have devoted all the time you can spare to the search engines, national directories and local listings, then you will have to find some more time to spare targeting the photography directories. With specialist interest directories there are two main types: those that look inward at other sites within that subject; and those that look out to promote their 'members' to the outside world.

The first group is very useful if you want to promote yourself among your peers. Sites with message boards, forums and chat rooms will benefit from lots of fellow photography enthusiasts coming to visit. In addition to providing directory listings, many operate a link exchange system where they will link to you, if you, in turn, link back to them. When you submit your details to these sites, they will ask you the exact URL of the page where you

intend to place the return link to them. This can be reason enough to include a smart 'Links' page on your site.

Why don't you create an advertisement for your own site? A simple graphic with your name and a statement about your work will do. There are a number of standard sizes for web adverts: the standard banner is 468 pixels wide by 60 pixels deep (the same size as the very first graphic you created for your logo in Chapter 7; see pages 80–81); a standard button measures 120 pixels wide by 90 pixels deep; the skyscraper-style adverts, which sit to the right of a scrollable page, are 120 wide and 600 pixels deep and are reported to be particularly effective.

By using an animated GIF file generator, you can introduce animation to these graphics. Several images are made to display in sequence and GIF generators can be found in some of the most advanced image-editing programs. There is a very basic GIF generator

The Internet Advertising Bureau has produced a brilliant guide to marketing online at www.iabuk.net. The site is updated regularly and provides information on the latest types of online advertising campaigns and assesses their effectiveness. You can see the specifications for all common advertisement formats here.

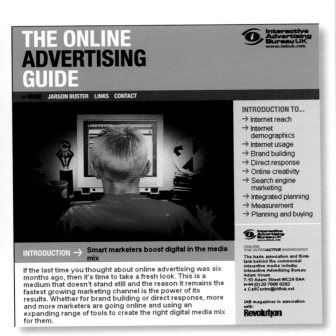

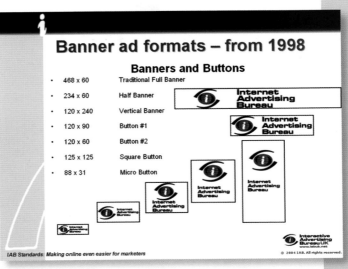

available from the download section of www.websitesforphotographers.co.uk. These images can be placed in a web page just like any image file. Use the generating program to create a loop of images. Different types of file can be imported and used as animation frames; all you need to do is make sure they are all the right size. Practise on your advertisement and experiment with animated GIFs for images in your own website.

You can send a banner or a button to each of the websites you swap links with, and, while you're at it, send copies to all the people you know who operate websites and who are prepared to display your ad for you. All the banners and buttons should be linked to your homepage. Of course, many sites will place your advert for payment, but you should apply the same considerations to these as to any paid directory entries you might consider. Is this site going to attract the kind of customers you want?

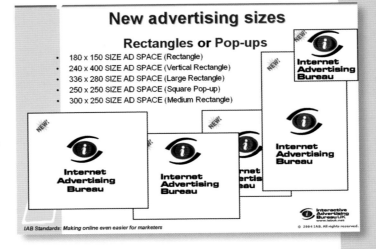

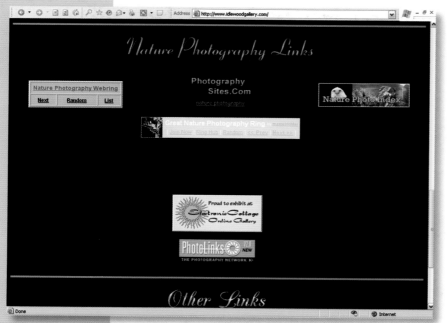

This site is a member of six webrings and displays all the graphics on its links page. The graphics appear when HTML code is added to the host page, creating the ring's links automatically.

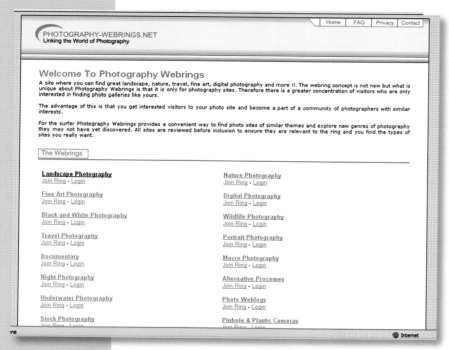

The homepage of a webring directory, showing the categories of photography sites. Webrings seldom reach out beyond the subject's community.

Advertising via webrings

There is also a type of web community that works a little bit like a specialist directory and uses the idea of exchanging links. This sort of community is known as a webring, and is probably the ultimate link exchange. You can find webrings dedicated to virtually every subject that you can imagine.

To join a webring, you agree to add links to it from a prominent part of your website – say, the bottom of the homepage. The link includes code and a banner from the owner or organizer of the webring. The banner announces that your site is a member of the community and has a link to a webring index page that lists all the other sites. Beside the banner is usually a pair of links that will take visitors straight to the next site in the 'ring', or the previous site. In this way, each of the sites promotes all of the others. A webring is an excellent way to promote your site to the online photography community, but it might not bring you very many clients.

Viral marketing

One of the most effective ways of marketing, one that was almost created by the web, is 'viral' marketing. This can be extremely powerful. The idea is that you create something to give away free on your website and then people pass it on to their friends. You should be relaxed about giving away images and the possibility that they might turn up on other sites without your permission.

The most common examples of this are desktop wallpaper – the images that people use to personalize their computer screen backgrounds – and screensavers. Desktop wallpaper is simply a JPEG image that fits the size and shape of a computer screen. Most of them are 800 x 600 pixels and 1024 x 768 pixels, and they should show your website address on them as a reminder to users as to where the image came from.

Screensavers can be made out of your images and displayed as a slideshow. The show can be set to music and even hyperlink to the website itself when the viewer clicks on a link. There is a simple screensaver maker available for you from the download section of the www.websitesforphotographers.co.uk website.

The key to getting the most from marketing in this way is encouraging visitors to download the wallpaper or screensaver and then either pass it on to others or tell them where they obtained it. If it is a desirable asset, friends will tell friends and your name will spread like wildfire. Have a look at the wallpaper that accompanies this book and website and imagine which has spread the word the fastest.

Keeping up with your customers

Let's imagine that you have got yourself listed on a couple of national and local directory sites, you joined a webring and all the important search engines know that you're there. Your message boards are gathering momentum and a photography magazine has recently voted your web pages 'photo site of the month'. Then you happen to be featured in a book like this one.

Within ten months, your site is attracting 1,500 visitors a day. Some of them want to tell you how much they like your work, others want to know how a particular picture was taken, and one visitor wants to know what lenses you use. Two people yesterday enquired about the possibility of you doing some work for them. If you get much more of this, your website will start to take over your life.

The first thing to do is go back to basics and redefine what it is you want your website to do. Clarify your aims and objectives. If the site has started to get out of hand, it might be time to reel it in a little, or pay someone else to take on part of the workload.

Sometimes a polite note will be enough to discourage enquiries that have become a burden. 'Unfortunately, Angus McOatup can't respond to all the messages generated by this website' might work. Alternatively, 'Inquiries about commissions and bookings are dealt with daily; all other messages will receive a response within ten working days' could be mercenary enough.

One man in America asks for five dollars for every technical question he answers. He makes this very clear

on his website and his email response has a reminder at the end. Most people are happy to pay him, even though he has no real way of enforcing the payment. Now that's a business model to consider, isn't it?

Cutting back might mean stopping some of the features of your site that helped make it successful in the first place, so you must exercise some discretion when choosing what to remove. If the work generated by the site is lucrative, then you simply need to get help. This might be in the form of an assistant; the cost-effectiveness considerations of hiring one is, unfortunately, beyond the scope of this book.

If you are selling photographic prints online and are struggling to meet orders, offload that site to a professional team and get yourself back in the darkroom. A site that requires lots of new content and is driven by special features may also need to be handed over to specialist web developers. A good professional will take on many of the customer service aspects of your website for you and become an intermediary between you and your online clients.

Any site that takes payment will need support from a third party and that's what we're going to look at next – the world of e-commerce.

This is one of several computer desktop wallpapers available for free from www.websitesforphotographers.co.uk. Wallpaper is simply an attractive image, representative of your work, created at a typical computer screen size. Common sizes are 800 x 600 and 1024 x 768 pixels. Image resolution is just 72dpi and JPEG compression should be as great as possible without compromising the quality of the image.

10 Making sales through the net

■ **If you intend to make sales through your website, you need to consider several things. How are you going to offer security to your customers? What is the best way to take the orders online? And just how do you get your money?**

E-commerce security issues

Successful web traders lead the way in e-commerce and security. Amazon has invested millions in addressing people's concerns about online shopping.

If you are selling goods or services online, you should never ask people to email their credit card details to you. It is amazing how many sites still do this, and how many people will put their credit card information into an email without a second thought. Email is one of the Internet's most insecure types of data transmission. Messages can go missing, be delivered to the wrong people, intercepted, scanned and generally abused by even the dumbest web criminals. Asking a customer to email a credit card number is like asking them to write it on a billboard. Don't do it.

There are many people who are still nervous about typing their credit card number into any web page, even the safest ones such as Amazon.com. Although the online book and music seller has been around since the late 1990s and has an excellent track record on payment security, some Internet users have not got the confidence to submit their credit card numbers. These are probably the same people who will allow their cards to be taken away from them for several minutes in a foreign restaurant and then sign a voucher with their number on it – a voucher that might be blowing around the dustbins behind the restaurant next morning.

Whether your customers are trusting and have confidence in security and honesty, or have a deep suspicion of all online traders, you might need to find a way of getting money off them. Any photographer selling work online needs to find a way to let their customers pay.

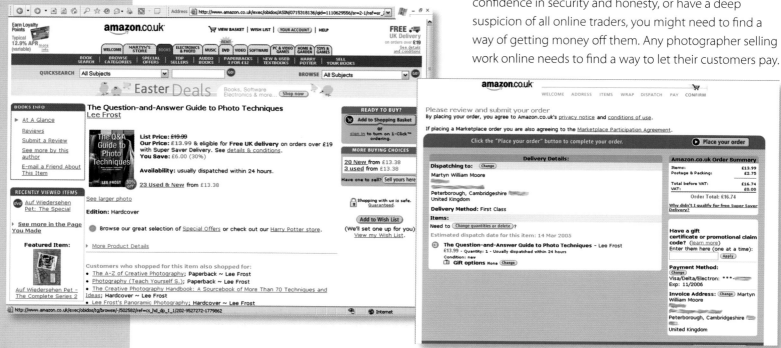

The padlock symbol that appears at the bottom right of your browser window and a web address that starts 'https:' indicate that the site uses secure encryption for processing payment data.

Online payments

Let's deal with the reluctant online payers first: offer an offline method of payment. If you have followed the advice about including real-world addresses and phone numbers, then anybody wanting to buy one of your limited edition prints can send you a cheque with their order, or telephone you and pay by credit card that way.

Now let's look at the various methods of secure online payments. Methods of payment via a web page rely on something known as encryption. This is a way of scrambling the data transmitted across the web in such a way that only the organization intended to receive the money can unscramble it. The most powerful form of encryption is known as 128-bit encryption and it is used as standard by all the big online retailers and banks. That is why Internet shopping is so safe.

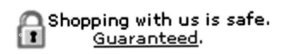

You can tell whether the site you are using is secure because you will get 'secure site' notices as you enter the safe area of the transaction pages. Also, a padlock icon will appear in the bottom right-hand corner of your browser window.

One area of growth in online payment is the ability to charge other types of account for online purchases.

For example, typing in the number of a mobile phone can add the charge to the customer's phone bill and the vendor receives payment from the phone service provider. Micropayments can be charged in this way, allowing a customer to buy cheap items online for the cost of a mobile text message. Online payments can be made via utility bills, too. You can, for example, buy your supermarket own-brand baked beans online and charge it to your gas bill. Some Internet banks can provide your business with these facilities.

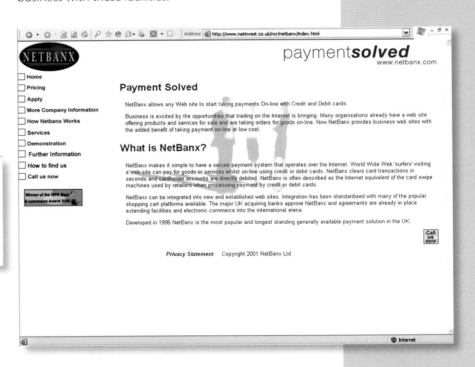

Netbanx is a dedicated online e-commerce facilitator. It has an enormous number of services, with new ideas emerging all the time.

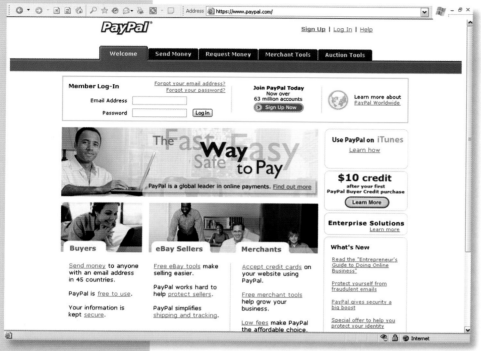

10

PayPal allows visitors to set up an account that can be used to pay for goods and services on hundreds of websites. When you want to sell somebody an image, they click through from your site to PayPal and make a payment to your account from theirs. All the major high-street banks provide online business services.

Online payment providers

There are many payment providers online. PayPal has established itself as just one of many reputable providers. Customers set up an account for themselves and then purchases from any PayPal-supported website can be charged to their account. PayPal then pays you. These services always make a small charge for this service at some point in the transaction, usually to you, the vendor.

The most common form of online payment is via the customer's credit card, typed into the vendor's web page, or a web page set up for the vendor by a payment provider. In order to offer this you need a merchant account with a bank. All major banks provide this service. Specialist Internet banks such as Netbanx can handle every aspect of online and electronic digital payment.

All these financial services will cost you money. You will pay to sell online. All the charges are clearly posted on websites and literature. Some are fixed monthly or annual charges, others may be based around paying per transaction. Choosing the payment structure that is right for you depends on the nature of the business you

want to do on the web. The online banks and finance companies will help you with this, and it is in their interest to advise you well. They stand to benefit themselves if your operation succeeds and they know you have a huge choice of suppliers.

Shopping carts

The best way to carry out a transaction with customers who want to order your photographs is by providing them with a 'shopping cart' feature. This system is popular on all kinds of online shopping sites. A good one will display an item, provide a description, show a photograph of the item, allow a buyer to add the item to their virtual trolley and proceed to the checkout. It will record their delivery details and credit card number – all securely protected by 128-bit encryption. Payment instructions are then forwarded to your merchant bank account and fulfilment details enable you to get the order out.

Shopping cart technology can be bought and incorporated into your site as long as your hosting service can handle it. You need it to provide a secure server if you

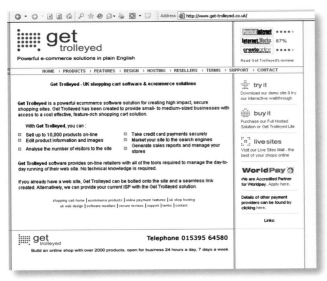

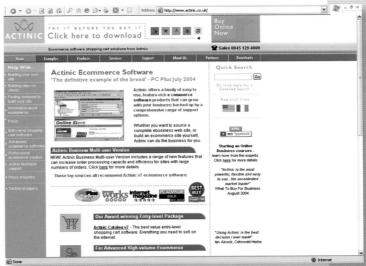

You can set up a shopping cart system that is hosted by someone else, such as Get Trolleyed. Your product images and words are loaded onto their site. Alternatively, you can build and host your own shopping cart site using software from companies such as Actinic.

are going to handle payments within your own site, but a shopping cart system can allow visitors to shop and add up their purchases before sending them to a third-party site to make a secure payment.

The software required to build the pages can be bought online and downloaded or installed from a CD and prices vary enormously. One of the most successful British shopping cart software packages comes from a company called Actinic. It has won industry and magazine accolades for its service. Shopping cart providers are listed at www.websitesforphotographers. co.uk, including services that offer the features free in return for advertising placed on the transaction pages. Some solutions even offer all the links to banking services built-in and some banks offer shopping cart features.

If you have progressed to creating your web pages using dedicated design software and have a good grasp of website structure and organization, then you can probably cope with bolting together a shopping cart section. Taking on the responsibility for placing all your stock online and selling it is not rocket science, but it is a big responsibility.

The time and effort required to maintain an e-commerce website while still finding time to be a photographer might make you decide to take your site to a professional web developer. That's what we look at next.

If you don't want to be involved in all the administration of selling your images directly, there is no shortage of agencies who will be happy to sell them for you. Proper Gander and Alamy are just two of many.

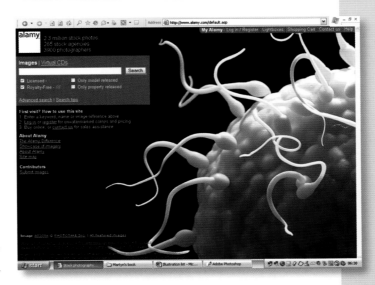

10 | Professional web building

At a certain point, your website might start to encroach on your professional life so much that you decide to enlist outside help. When it's time to reclaim your life as a photographer, rather than as a website manager, you might need to approach a web developer. However, you might have so enjoyed the experience of setting up and running a website that you go further down this path to become a professional web builder yourself. We explore both routes in this section.

It's a jungle out there, although if you look closely, this jungle has all been grown by one designer. Steven Booth created the website for this book. The UK Web Design Association (right) is just one place where you will find a good designer.

When it's time to get outside help

So you wake up one morning and you are scared to look at your emails. Yesterday, you had thirty orders for your landscape collection and by 11pm last night, you'd only printed up nineteen sets. It's time to get a darkroom assistant or find a commercial lab that takes as much care in the darkroom as you do.

Or you wake up one morning and daren't turn on your mobile phone. Yesterday you were interrupted four times during the shoot at the water works and missed a great commission when you turned it off at the town hall presentation. It's time to hire somebody to take your calls and manage your diary.

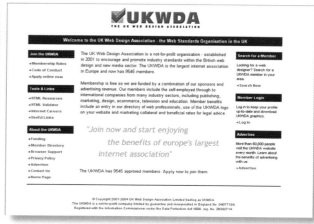

Clikpic offers simple design, content management and hosting for an all-in price. The first website that we looked at in detail, Tim Sandall's (see page 56), was created with Clikpic.

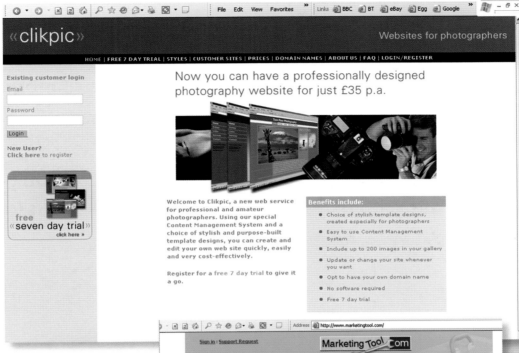

Web designers, photographers, illustrators... is there anybody out there not involved in media creation? The United States has no shortage of digital artists, as this directory shows.

And Angus, the small animals section of your website is attracting so much traffic, the Arbroath web agency wants to sell advertising on it. They think that a cats section would be even more successful, Mr McOatup. Time to create a gallery that has nothing to do with growing your core business.

When the managing of a web business starts to get in the way of the work that you need to be doing as a photographer, it is time to consider handing the work over to the professionals.

Choosing a web developer

Several factors need to be taken into consideration when you are choosing a web developer. First of all, the number of developers working in rural communities, for example, is still relatively small, so when it comes to choice, you might not have much. However, the online world is not really ruled by geography. There is no real need for you to be within twenty minutes of the person who designs and hosts your website – she or he could be on the other side of the world.

Choosing your web developer takes us back to the points that were made in the early chapters of this book. You need to decide exactly what you need, what you want, and what you would quite like if they can manage it for the price. And because you've read the most helpful web development book on the market, you will be able to meet your techie wizards on much more even terms. You know how you feel about sophisticated Flash intro movies; you know you absolutely do not want background music or the sound of a camera shutter clattering away; you know how long a 300k image can take to download and you know how much is a reasonable price to pay for web development. Be warned; some web designers will love clients like you, but others might not.

Find out if the person running the company is genuinely passionate about the medium. Many web agencies were started by entrepreneurs who might otherwise have been selling conservatories or running a telemarketing operation from an industrial unit. That's not to say a company like that won't give you good service, but you might feel happier working with someone who is a genuine web evangelist. And while the techie geek is a creature we know and love, if he answers all your telephone calls in a bizarre hybrid language that combines English with smatterings of JavaScript and HTML code, you might start to feel uncomfortable.

The business-driven agency will offer you an 'exciting' range of website features designed to relieve you of the largest amount of money for the smallest amount of work. The geek-driven operation will be looking to sell you cutting-edge technology (maybe stuff that they have been dying to try for months) that you probably don't need and that will either never be finished, or never work.

These are two horrible generalizations, of course, but they give you an idea of the typical traits to look out for. The people to track down are real people, who want

Web designers often have the simplest sites. This could be because they are too busy designing other people's sites to spend much time on their own, or it could be that they value clarity and ease of use for their own site and show off their more spectacular talents in the work they do for clients.

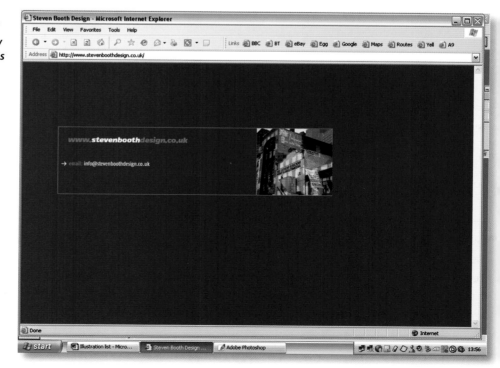

to understand your business, your objectives and your problems and who are thrilled that you have acquired a good understanding of how the Internet works. When you find these people, tell them to tell all their clients about this book.

Dealing with web designers

Whenever you deal with web designers, always be clear about exactly what you're getting for your money. As when you're dealing with a builder or heating engineer, get a written itemized quote for everything. The arrangement should be: 'You're doing all of this, for this amount of money. Anything else you do will not be paid for unless we agree it first. And you need to do all of this, unless you have a better idea, but we will need to agree that, too. What will happen if you don't finish it on time? Can we discuss compensation?' If they don't run away or start to hurl abuse, you might be okay.

Ask for mock-ups or layouts and explanations of navigation. You shouldn't have to pay extra to be shown what you're going to get for your money.

Find out how thorough their testing is and does everything they create work on every type of browser on all types of computer. Practise this line: 'What's your attitude to consistent cross-platform functionality?' That should scare them.

When you find the right people to take on the running of your website, you can go back to doing what you do best – taking pictures. Let somebody else worry about compressing images to the optimum quality/file size settings and uploading a new gallery of your latest work – you've got clients to meet and art to create.

Don't ignore your website, though. Even if you have handed it over to somebody else to manage day to day, you should still keep in touch with web developments and review your own needs twice a year. Having a great website can take your work out to the world and bring the world to you with work. Having a website is an essential component of many successful business strategies, and this book has shown you how to start making it a part of yours.

Web building yourself

You took up photography in the first place because you wanted to express yourself; you enjoyed the technology that it employs or maybe you wanted to communicate visually with others. In these digital days, many people have received the same kind of satisfaction from computers and the worldwide web. The Internet is a subject that draws you in; it is easy to become obsessed and even addicted.

Then one day a friend says: 'Will you build me a website, please? Just a simple one… I'm happy to pay you.' You need to stop and think: 'Can I? Should I? Which of the "web experts to avoid" will I become?'

Dipping your toe into web building for others could mark the start of a whole new chapter in your life. There's a lot more to learn before you can offer a good professional service and the technology moves at an extremely fast rate. But there are worse ways of earning a living, and then you will only drag your camera kit to the top of mountains in the pouring rain if you really want to.

Back in 1998, just after the birth of his second child, a middle-aged, part-time photographer built himself a website to help pass the sleepless nights. The site offered his services and he sent details of it to all the search engines. The site was awful, but it had a visitor counter and the number kept going up.

By the end of the year, he had built a site for a fellow journalist and started one for a local charity. In 1999 he created a website for his sister's business and another for a motorcycle tuning company. He also wrote an article on web design for a new magazine he had helped to create: *Digital Photo*. Throughout 1999 he edited *Internet Magazine* and was on the judging panels for some of Britain's most prestigious web design awards. In 2001, he helped launch one of the world's biggest motoring websites. Late in 2004, he decided to write a low-tech book to help other photographers become web-savvy. The aim of the book was to show photographers how easy it is to create a website and take their work and businesses online.

You've just read that book.

Your online resource

See the examples shown in this book, and more besides, in a live online environment at www.websitesforphotographers.co.uk.

The site of the book was built while the book was being written. Now that the book is finished, a lot of time is being spent making sure that the site conforms to (most of) the advice given in the book! Therefore don't be surprised if the site doesn't look exactly like the pictures you see here.

Links are provided to the software needed to carry out many of the tasks mentioned in the book. They are changed and added to as new products and services become available. In this way, the site behaves like a live appendix to the book.

Perhaps the most exciting part of the website is the templates section. Designer Steven Booth has created several website and gallery templates for you to download to your computer and then add your own images and text. If you're not a great designer or don't want to hire one just yet, that shouldn't stop you having a great-looking website!

The way the templates work is simple. They all have written instructions included in the download, but the basic idea is that you download a template as a zipped file. Its contents are unzipped into a working folder that becomes your Publish folder.

Next, you work your way through all the components that Steven has created, looking at web page files with an HTML editor (there's a free one on the website) and opening the image files with an image editor (there's a free one of those as well!).

All the text on the web page can be edited to say whatever you want it to say and the sample graphic logos can be replaced with logos created using the techniques described in this book (see pages 80–81).

Replace the sample images in the templates with your own images. Your images will have to be optimized for the web – but you have already learned how to do that

The website's homepage provides information for visitors who have found the site via links and search engines. It introduces this book, provides an opportunity to buy it and explains how the site and book work together to create a unique multimedia resource.

One of the most exciting aspects to *The Photographer's Guide to Setting Up a Website* is the unique and dedicated website that accompanies the book. Just in case you missed the many references to the address throughout the book, it's www.websitesforphotographers.co.uk.

This is the place to go to see the example one-page site and three-page site in their glowing luminosity. The featured photographers' websites look bigger and brighter, too, and really should be enjoyed in their intended medium. The site has links to all the websites mentioned in the book and several other excellent examples that had to be omitted due to space constraints. You can watch photographers' sites evolve, too. Some even changed during the time the book was being written.

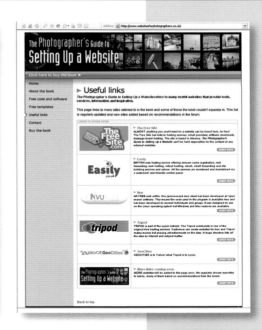

(see pages 66–67). The gallery templates use two versions of each photo – one for the small thumbnail view and one for the bigger display.

The trick is to replace each sample image with one of your own photos but keep the image dimensions and file names the same as the samples. If each sample is replaced by one of your own photos, the gallery will work in exactly the way Steven created it, but featuring your photos. It is vital that the replacement photos are placed in the appropriate folder in relation to the other files. They must also use the same naming convention as that created by Steven and they should be created to the same widths and heights as the samples.

All of the resources available at www. websitesforphotographers.co.uk. have been carefully checked for bugs and viruses. However, some of the downloads come from the developers' own sites and *The Photographer's Guide to Setting Up a Website* cannot be held responsible for the content. Your security and privacy online is your responsibility and the use of up-to-date virus and spyware protection is strongly recommended. There are links to protective software on the site.

In the Contact section of the site you can find out a little bit more about the team behind the book. It

isn't possible to answer every message that comes in via this page and the team is not able to solve your technical problems on an individual basis. However, the Internet community is very good at helping itself and to encourage this the site has its own forum, which can be accessed from the Contact page. This is the place to go to comment on the book, comment on the website, discuss the issues raised by *The Photographer's Guide to Setting Up a Website* and ask advice from fellow forum visitors. If you think you can help someone else on the forum, go ahead.

We encourage free speech on the forum and we value all feedback. At launch, the forum will not be moderated, so we ask that you respect other users of the forum and adopt basic standards of fairness and decency when you use it. Having said that, we're also obliged to point out that the views expressed on the forum are not necessarily those of the author and publisher of *The Photographer's Guide to Setting Up a Website* and we cannot be held responsible for the comments posted. Technical advice given by members of the forum has not been checked by the publishing team and is followed at your own risk. *The Photographer's Guide to Setting Up a Website* cannot be held responsible for any outcome of following advice posted on the forum. It's a shame to have to say all that, but there you go…

The website provides you with useful templates to adapt for your own site, along with links to the sites illustrated in the book and other useful ones not mentioned. Developments move rapidly and this is the best way to keep up to date. Join the website forum section and share your experience if you have found a website or product that has helped you, or can offer advice to others.

Glossary

Acrobat: Free Adobe software for viewing PDFs with images and text.

Active Server Page (ASP): Web pages generated from assets in a database by a site using active server page technology. These pages do not exist as normal or 'flat' HTML, but are called up by the site and created on demand. Java server pages work in a similar way using the .jsp suffix on page files.

ActiveX: Microsoft technology that allows small programs to run inside the user's web browser adding functionality.

Adobe: Software manufacturer, perhaps best known for its industry-standard image editor Photoshop and widely used document format PDF. More information at: www.adobe.com.

ADSL: Asymmetric Digital Subscriber Line – another name for a broadband, or high-speed, Internet connection. Downloading is usually faster than uploading.

Adware: A form of spyware, usually unwelcome, that installs programs to generate advertising on the user's computer (often pop-up windows).

Alt tag: The text that appears when the cursor moves over a picture. This is the alt tag in HTML and is useful for people who view pages in text-only mode, or who have visual impairments.

Animated GIF: A GIF is a type of image file. When it is animated, it might flash or show a moving picture. It is made up of a number of still images displayed in succession like a flipbook.

Anti-virus: Software that helps protect the user's computer from viruses, filtering emails and scanning downloads looking for known harmful files.

Apple Macintosh: Alternative computer and operating system (OS) to the much more common PC (Microsoft Windows-based). Also called Macintosh computers, 'Macs' are favoured by publishers and photo/image 'creatives'.

Application: Another name for a computer program used to do a specific job. Microsoft Word is a word processing application.

Attachment: A file 'attached' to and sent with a text email message. Often, photographs or word documents are attached to emails.

Avatar: An image of the user or a favourite character used to represent someone in games or chat forums on the web.

Bandwidth: The amount of data that can be carried by an Internet connection. Measured in kilobytes per second (kbps).

Banner: A rectangular-shaped advert or bar normally at the top of a web page. Traditionally 468 pixels wide by 60 pixels deep.

Bitmap: An image file format. Files have the suffix .bmp.

Blog: From WeB LOG – an online personal diary with links to other websites that the author likes.

Bookmark/Favourite: A website can be 'bookmarked' or added to a list of 'favourites' in the user's browser. When they want to go back to that page, they can go there in one click instead of trying to remember the site's address.

bps: Bytes per second. The measurement of how fast data can be transmitted over a telephone line or on a network connection.

Broadband: A high-speed Internet connection. Usually refers to ADSL, which is ten times faster than the 56k phone modem and is 'always on'. At home, it allows telephone calls to be made or received when the user is connected to the Internet. Other broadband connections include cable, satellite and wireless.

Browser: A program used to view web pages and 'browse' websites. Netscape Navigator and Internet Explorer are the most popular browsers. There are several smaller independent browsers such as Mozilla Firefox. A Macintosh computer can use these browsers and its own brand: Safari.

Bugs: Errors in software or web pages that can make them work erratically.

Button ad: A square-shaped button-style advertisement. Traditionally 120 pixels wide by either 60 or 90 pixels deep.

Byte: Bytes are used to measure amounts of computer data. One byte is roughly the same as one character of text. One Kb (kilobyte or K) is approximately 1000 bytes, one Mb (megabyte) is approximately 1000Kb, and one Gb (gigabyte) is approximately 1000Mb.

Cache: The user's browser uses a 'cache' to store web pages they have seen already. When they go back to those pages they'll load more quickly because they come from the cache and don't need to be downloaded again. Copies of web pages are also stored in online caches between the original web server and the user's connection, so they may have to wait until these caches have refreshed before they can see updated versions of web pages. See Proxy Server.

CGI: Common Gateway Interface. A script used in web pages and processed on the web server that allows them to have order forms, searchable databases and chat forums.

Chat: Real-time chat where users type in a window and other users can reply instantly. Chat normally involves several people. Direct chatting between two devices is Instant Messaging.

Compression: The process of reducing the size of computer files by electronically 'squeezing' them so that they can move around the Internet more quickly. Zip files are a common example of one type of compression. JPEGs are compressed image files.

Cookie: A file placed on the computer's hard drive by websites so the sites can recognize them the next time they visit.

Copyright, Design and Patents Act, 1988: British legislation that protects authors' and artists' copyright and governs the use and reproduction of their work.

Data Protection Act: A law that protects personal information stored about customers and visitors to websites. The law gives them the right to see data held about them and prevent it being passed on without their permission.

Database: Information stored in tables. It can be searched, sorted and used in different ways using database programs.

Directory: A folder where a computer stores other files and information. In a URL such as www.websitesforphotographers.co.uk/downloads 'downloads' is a directory.

DNS: Domain Name Server system that changes a website address like: www.davidandcharles.co.uk (easy for humans to use) into a numbered IP address like 213.253.134.7 (easy for computers to use).

Domain name: The people-friendly name for a website that is converted to an IP address by the Domain Name Server (DNS). The domain name is the part before the forward slash.

Download: Transferring a file onto the user's computer from another computer on the Internet.

Drag and drop: Clicking on an icon or selection, holding the mouse button down and moving the mouse to 'drag' the selection to a new location. When the button is released the item is 'dropped'.

Dreamweaver: Web page editor from software developer Macromedia, part of the Studio MX suite of programs.

Drop-down: Often used to describe an action on a program or web page. For example, drop-down menus.

E-commerce: Buying and selling goods and services over the Internet.

Emoticons: Facial expressions created using text. For example, winking ;-) or smiling :-) can be used to say 'don't take that too seriously'. Also known as 'Smilies'.

Encryption: Encoding process used to stop unauthorized people accessing the user's private information when it is sent over the Internet. The most secure sites on the Internet use 128-bit encryption. Encrypted sites display a padlock in the corner of the browser window.

Error message: Displayed by the computer when something has gone wrong. There will often be an explanation including an 'error code' that may be useful when seeking help.

Executables: File containing a program, for example, files that end in the extension '.exe'. These files have access to important parts of the computer and will trigger warnings from anti-virus software.

FAQ: Frequently Asked Questions. A list of standard answers to questions that newcomers to your website may have. If your site attracts the same questions over and over again, this might be a worthwhile addition to save having to reply to the same queries over and over again.

File extension: Letters after the full stop at the end of the file name. They tell the computer which program to use when opening the file. Common extensions in web-type files are .htm and .html for web pages and .gif and .jpg for image files.

Firewall: Protective security program that sits between the user's computer and the Internet and watches for hacking, viruses or unapproved data transfer.

Flame: Usually a response to another post on a message board that the 'flamer' finds offensive.

Flash: A Macromedia plug-in that users download to allow their browser to show Flash and Shockwave animations on websites (these are usually pre-installed with the most popular browsers).

FOLDOC: Free On-Line Dictionary Of Computing edited by Denis Howe and available at http://foldoc.doc.ic.ac.uk/.

Font: Typefaces used on-screen and in print documents or on websites. Some of the most frequently used are Times New Roman, Arial and Courier.

Frames: Frames allow several pages to be displayed in one window at the same time. Users can click on a link in one frame and see the linked page appear in another frame.

Freeware: Software programs that are available for free. Sometimes the software is a trial version and 'free' for only a limited amount of time or some of the features of the full version are disabled. There may also be a commercial reason for making the software available. Advertising messages may be carried and sometimes spyware is installed on the user's machine.

FrontPage: Microsoft's web page creation and editing program. Part of the Office suite of applications.

FTP: File Transfer Protocol. A system used to upload files to and download files from computers on the Internet.

Gallery: A way of displaying images in a website. Often uses thumbnails linked to bigger versions with 'next' and 'back' buttons to allow visitors to look through the bigger versions.

GIF: Type of compressed image file. GIF files work best for non-photo images such as logos and line drawings due to a reduced range of colours.

Gigabyte: One thousand million bytes (1000Mb).

Hacking: Unauthorized access to a computer, its files and programs by a 'hacker' – someone who can break through computer security systems.

History: A list of websites visited by a browser over a period of time: today, yesterday, last week, two weeks ago, etc.

Hits: Misused term for the number of times a web page has been visited. Some web stats count every file downloaded as a 'hit', so a single page with four images in it would register five hits, one for each image and one for the page itself. A more useful term is 'page impressions', which gives a true indication of the popularity of a page within a site.

Homepage: The 'front' or index page of a website. This usually tells visitors what is on the site, how to get around it and how to search for things that will interest them.

Host: The computer or 'server' on which the actual website is stored. This computer is usually owned by and leased from the hosting company.

HTML: Hypertext Markup Language – the language in which web pages are written. It is actually a fairly straightforward code with some common and easily learned 'tags' or commands. You can view the HTML of any web page by choosing 'Source' from the 'View' menu of the web browser when that page is displayed.

HTTP: Hypertext Transfer Protocol. The letters, usually in lower case, at the start of a website address on the worldwide web.

Hyperlink: Technical name for a link on a web page. Clicking on one takes the visitor to another page or Internet file. The mouse pointer changes to a hand shape when passing over a hyperlink to show that it may be clicked.

Hypertext: Text arranged in a non-linear fashion that the visitor can move through by clicking on links. For example, text that mentions Nikon cameras may contain hyperlinks to separate text that gives more information about Nikon cameras, itself with links to other new text areas and also back to the original text.

Icon: A small picture that, when users click on it, launches an application, program or link on the worldwide web.

Image map: An image divided into a number of areas called 'hot spots', which are hyperlinks. Users know the hot spots are there because the mouse pointer changes to a hand shape when passing over them.

ImageReady: Adobe Image-editing software, often used in conjunction with Photoshop to optimize images for use on the web.

Installing: Adding a program to a user's computer hard disk so they can use it. Installation is usually started by clicking on a file called 'setup.exe' on Windows and shown by a diamond/arrow icon on a Macintosh. The most common ways to install programs are from CD-ROM or via an Internet download.

Instant messaging: Chatting online via a special application called an Instant Messenger (IMs). IMs have a buddy list that tells users when people they know are online.

Internet: Millions of computers around the world connected together by cables, telephone lines or satellites and sharing data.

Internet Explorer: The most popular browser, designed by Microsoft and pre-installed on virtually all Windows-based PCs.

Intranet: A company's internal website used for communicating between staff, hosted on an internal network and not accessible from outside the organization.

IP address: The numerical address of every computer on the Internet. Unique, like a phone number, and with only four billion of them we are running out!

IRC: Internet Relay Chat. A real-time chat system using a program where comments are typed in a chat window.

ISP: Internet Service Provider. An ISP is a company that provides Internet connections to private and business customers, for example, AOL, Demon Internet, BT Openworld.

Java: A programming language widely used on the web to run small programs in the user's browser called applets.

JavaScript: A scripting language used in the code of a web page to do things like change graphics when the mouse passes over them, make new browser windows 'pop up', bookmark a page with one click or send the page to a friend.

JPEG: A common type of image file that is good for saving photos and other images with many different colours. It uses 'lossy' compression to reduce file size, meaning that the more the image is compressed the more quality is reduced as data is 'lost'. JPEG stands for Joint Photographic Experts Group – the developers of the format.

LAN: Local Area Network. A network usually (but not always) within an office, building or closed geographical area.

Layers: A useful feature in Photoshop that allows images to be laid on top of each other and edited independently. When a final, single image is required, these layers can be 'flattened'.

Link: Words or pictures that visitors can click on that take them from one place (an Internet page, email message etc.) to somewhere else (another page, a picture etc.).

Logging in: Using a username and password to prove your identity so you can access documents on a computer, an Internet connection or a registered user-only area on a website.

Macro: Record and save a series of commands so they can be reapplied later with a single command or keyboard stroke.

Macromedia: Developer of web, image and animation tools and software. Macromedia STUDIO MX includes Dreamweaver, Flash, Fireworks and FreeHand. More information at www.macromedia.com. Merged with Adobe in 2005.

Mailing list: Messages and replies that are distributed to all the people subscribing to the particular mailing list. Big email communications where everybody on the list can take part. Most commercial messages sent to mailing lists do not allow members to see the details of other members.

Malware: Malicious software, like Spyware, developed to harm a computer system, launch a virus, steal credit card details or launch undesirable web pages.

Megabytes: A measure of information quantity equal to 1000 kilobytes (one million bytes).

Memory: The storage and thinking parts of the computer. More storage memory on the hard disk (ROM) means you can save more files and more thinking memory (RAM) means the computer can think about several problems at once.

Message boards: Web pages containing 'threads' or strings of messages posted by visitors to the page. Most require users to register before posting. Message boards are monitored by moderators who remove offensive postings.

Meta search engine: A web search engine that automatically submits the user's search request to several search engines at the same time and then comes back with the results after only a few seconds. Well-known examples include MetaCrawler and Ask Jeeves.

Metadata: Information about a web page hidden inside its HTML code (between metatags) to help search engines find it. It often includes a description of the page, which will be picked up by search engines.

MHz: Megahertz. A measurement of processing speed. The more MHz, the faster the computer can perform a calculation.

MIME: A standard for encoding information other than text so that it can be attached to an email and sent across the Internet.

Mirror: A copy of a website held on a different server to speed up download times by reducing the congestion from many users accessing just one site at the same time. Also known as load balancing.

Modem: The hardware that connects users' computers to the Internet or to other computers around the world. Some are inside the user's computer (internal) and some are separate boxes outside the user's computer (external).

Montage: A collection of pictures brought together in an image or web page editor to make one single image file or give the impression of one image.

Movie intro: A short animated film, often created with Flash, that introduces a website. Can be slow to load and should be accompanied by a 'skip intro' link for visitors in a hurry.

MP3: A digital audio format that allows CD tracks to be reduced to around a tenth of their normal size without a significant loss of quality – from, say, 35Mb down to 3Mb.

MPEG: A standard used for compressing video and audio files. The popular MPEG1 Audio Layer (or mp3) format is popular for distributing music on the Internet.

Multimedia: The combination of different types of media such as audio, video and text.

Navigation bar: A set of links to the main sections of a website that appears on each web page within that website. The navigation bar often appears at the top or left of a web page.

Netiquette: Unofficial etiquette governing online behaviour. For example, no CAPITALS because they indicate shouting, and no advertising except in designated areas.

Netscape Navigator: A popular web browser designed by Netscape Communications Corporation. It is the main competitor to Microsoft's Internet Explorer.

Network: A group of computers communicating with each other via a server along cables or wirelessly.

Newbie: Someone who is new to the Internet or a part of the Internet, for example, a 'chat newbie'.

Newsgroups: Forums for exchanging information and views over the Internet that are held on newsgroup servers. Often accessed via email programs such as Microsoft Outlook/ Outlook Express or Entourage. When users post a message, it is systematically copied to other newsgroup servers around the world so other people can read it and reply with their views.

Nvu: Pronounced 'new view'. Free 'open source' web editor, available to download from www.nvu.com or via www. websitesforphotographers.co.uk .

Open source: Software, usually free, with code that is publicly available to all. The IT community for the wider community, profit-free or supported through voluntary donations, develops these applications.

Operating system: The software environment on a computer. The most famous ones are Windows, Linux and Mac OS.

Optimization: Normally associated with the processing of images to make them suitable for use in web pages. An optimized image is converted to 'RGB' format, 'resampled' to 72 dots per inch and adjusted to the desired size. A simple graphic, such as a logo, will be saved as a GIF file. A high-quality image, such as a photograph, will be saved as a JPEG and have a degree of compression applied.

Packet: Data sent over the Internet is divided up into lots of small packets of information that are then reassembled in the correct order at the other end.

Page impressions: A measure of traffic to and around a website. One visitor downloading one page to view on their computer creates one page impression. This is often confused with the more vague term 'hits'. Page impressions, unique users and session times are the most useful website traffic statistics.

Page not found: Error message that users see when they enter an incorrect website address or an address for a site that has subsequently moved.

Paint Shop Pro: A commercial software program used to create, edit and save images. Developed by Jasc, now owned by Corel. Similar functionality to Adobe Photoshop but cheaper.

Password: A series of letters, numbers and characters used to access a computer, Internet connection, email or websites that the user has registered with.

PC: Personal Computer. PC has now been accepted as referring to machines built around a specification devised by IBM and normally using the Microsoft Windows operating system rather than Apple Macintosh computers.

PDA: Personal Digital Assistant. A pocket-sized computer.

PDF: Portable Document Format. These files will print exactly as they appear on screen. Users need the free Adobe Acrobat Reader program (which is available to download from www.adobe.com) to open a PDF file.

Photoshop: A commercial software package from Adobe used to design, produce and alter images for use on websites or in print. Photoshop is generally accepted as the industry-standard imaging software application.

Pixel: The smallest resolvable part of a digital image. A dot, basically. For web use, a colour pixel is made up of red, blue and green elements; it has a value for brightness and can even be transparent. Because computer screens almost always use a resolution of 72 dots per inch, pixels can be used as a unit of measurement in web design and to express the size of online images.

Platform: The type of computer being used and its operating system. Common platforms include the IBM-based PC with Microsoft Windows and the Apple Macintosh computer with Mac OS.

Plug-in: A mini program that adds extra functions to a program that has already been installed. Without it, a site that requires those downloads won't fully work. Internet plug-ins for web browsers include Macromedia's Flash, Real Player and Apple's QuickTime. Plug-ins will also add new features to image-editing programs like Photoshop.

POP: Short for Post Office Protocol. The current technical standard for retrieving emails from an ISP's mail server.

Portal: A website that acts as a gateway to the Internet by directing visitors to information elsewhere. Directory sites can act as themed portals. Parts of the website at www.websitesforphotographers.co.uk work like a portal for photographers interested in websites by gathering together lots of different websites with a common theme.

Protocol: A set of rules that tells two or more computers how to transfer data.

Proxy server: A computer owned by an ISP that stores copies of popular web pages. This means that when a visitor tries to view certain pages, rather than going to the original web server of the web page the visitor's computer retrieves it from the proxy. This loads pages more quickly. See also 'Cache'.

QuickTime: A popular format from Apple for streaming audio and video on the web. Users need a QuickTime multimedia player to view or listen to QuickTime clips.

RealPlayer: A popular format from Real.com for streaming audio and video on the web. Users need a RealOne player to view or listen to RealPlayer clips. RealAudio is 'streamed' in a similar way to radio broadcasts, meaning that the clip can be played as it is downloaded.

Refresh/Reload: The command under the View menu of a browser or button used to download a web page again. In Internet Explorer it's called 'Refresh' and in Netscape Navigator 'Reload'.

Registration: Signing up to a website for access to 'members only' content or to be added to a mailing list. Registration requires users to submit an email address and choose an available username and password. Some systems email a random-generated password to the user, who can then use it to log on and change the password to one more memorable.

Repeat visits: Part of web stats reporting that reveals how many times a visitor will return to a site in a given time period; usually per week or per month.

Resampling: Processing an image in an image-editing application to change the resolution and dimensions and retain the optimum image quality for those settings.

RGB: Red, Green and Blue. A combination of these colours in various proportions will make any colour. Image files for the web should be in RGB format, printed images are normally in CMYK (cyan, magenta, yellow and black) format.

Robot: A software tool for performing automated tasks, often on the Internet. For example, 'spiders' or search bots are used by search engines to automatically scour the web and populate their databases.

Scanner: A device that scans images and converts them into a digital format that the computer can then process. Scanned images can be 'optimized' and added to web pages.

Search engine: A website that allows visitors to search the Internet for information. The search engine lists results that relate to the user's search phrase.

Secure: A method of sending or storing information that is 'encrypted' or security protected to prevent unauthorized users from accessing it.

Server: A powerful computer that holds data to be shared over a network or over the Internet. When users view a web page it is being sent to them by a server.

Session times: The length of time visitors spend on a website per visit. A useful part of web stats reporting that indicates how interesting or 'sticky' a website is. Any website that retains its visitors for more than four to five minutes is doing well in this fast-moving world.

Shareware: Software that is free or almost free to try out. Shareware often has a 'free trial' period for users to test the program. After this, payment is required, but it is usually quite cheap.

Shockwave: A Macromedia plug-in that gives users access to interactive multimedia on the Internet. Often used to make CD-ROMs, it can be used to combine animation, video and audio.

Shopping cart: The Internet equivalent of a shopping trolley. Items can be added to the 'cart' while a user browses online items for sale. The user then clicks through to the website's 'checkout' section, where items are listed, the cost is calculated, the delivery address is confirmed and payment processed.

Signature file: A small file of text that can be automatically added to every email message sent. It contains the user's name and email address, but may also include the user's job title or a favourite quote. Sometimes called a '.sig'.

Site plan: A sketch, map or graphical representation of a website. May be created prior to building the site to show sections, pages and links.

Skyscraper ad: Tall ad usually positioned to the right of a web page. Typically 160 pixels wide by 600 pixels high (deep).

SMTP: Simple Mail Transfer Protocol. The Internet protocol for the sending and receiving of email over the Internet.

Software: The programs such as the operating system and word processors, email applications or Internet browsers that run on the hardware – the computer.

Source code: The code a web page is written in. This is usually HTML but may also involve CGI, Java or JavaScript. Users can view the source code of a web page by clicking on the 'View Source' menu option in their browser.

Spam: Bulk junk email sent to many people at once, usually involving advertising or offering services. Filtering services are available and some email programs can be taught to recognize the type of mail the user considers junk.

Splash page: A web page that the visitor sees while the rest of a website is loading. It is usually an animated design and often offers the visitor the choice of 'skipping' this intro or watching the rest of the movie.

Spyware: Software that is installed on the user's computer, often without them realizing, that sends information on the user's software and Internet usage to outside companies. Often downloaded at the same time as 'free' software.

Sticky sites: Popular websites that visitors spend a lot of time at. Sticky sites have engaging content and often encourage repeat visits.

Streaming: A sound or video file that is played at almost the same time it is being sent from a website, saving the user time not having to wait for the entire file to download.

StuffIt: Macintosh software used for compressing files (making them take up less memory), thereby making them quicker to send over the Internet. StuffIt files have the file extension .sit.

Tags: Found in the HTML code for a webpage that defines attributes such as the way words, pictures and other content appear on the page.

TCP/IP: The combination of protocols that make the Internet work. TCP deals with dividing data into 'packets' of information. IP deals with passing these packets from one computer to the next until they reach their final destination.

Thread: A string of messages, often email messages or message board posts, linked by a common subject – the online equivalent of a conversation. Message boards thread messages on the same subject together.

Three Click Rule: Web design mantra that states that every page on a website should be no more than three clicks from every other page. Requires careful planning and clarity of navigation.

Thumbnail: A very small version of an image, often in a gallery. Usually clicks through to a larger version.

Trial software: Software that will work for a limited time. If users decide to purchase it they can obtain a registration code that they type into the software to make it work permanently.

Trojan: A harmless-looking program that carries with it viruses, worms or another program that will damage the user's computer. Often distributed as an email attachment.

Unique users: Individual visitors to a website often identified by their IP address. This figure can be distorted when home users access a site regularly. Each time they log on, their ISP will allocate a different IP address to them, so they appear in site stats as different users. Conversely, corporate visitors on a network will share a common IP address, so many visitors from the same company will only show on site stats as one.

UNIX: A computer operating system (OS) used by most Internet service providers (ISPs) on their 'host' computers. Other systems will allow many people to connect to the same resources at one time, but Unix is better for certain tasks.

URL: Uniform Resource Locator. The techie term for the address of a website or document on the web.

Username: The name by which a registered user is known to a computer, an Internet access account or a website. Often the first part of an email address, the part before the @ sign.

Virus: Pieces of code that are designed to reproduce and damage data or system performance. The growing number of viruses makes anti-virus software protection essential.

WAP: Wireless Application Protocol. A technology that allows users to access basic information on the Internet from a mobile phone or PDA, including email, sport, weather, traffic and news.

Web editor: Software for designing web pages without necessarily knowing HTML, the code that makes up web pages work. Often as easy to use as word processors.

Web server: A powerful computer permanently connected to the Internet that 'serves' web pages and other Internet files stored on it to users.

Web space: The space on a web server that is allocated by an ISP for a customer to put a website on. Most Internet service providers now allocate free web space for their customers.

Web stats: Figures representing the amount of traffic to and around a website. Typically measured in page impressions, unique users, session times and repeat visits.

Web traffic: Term used to describe data travelling around the Internet. The Internet can sometimes slow down because of the amount of traffic. Traffic to a website is measured in page impressions, unique users and session times.

Webcam: An inexpensive, simple video camera that can sit on top of the user's monitor or pointed at something interesting. It's designed to send video or still pictures over the Internet. The image from a webcam can be embedded into a web page.

Webmail: Email accessed through a web page rather than via a dedicated email program. Hotmail is a well-known example of a webmail service.

Webmaster: The person in charge of a website. Probably you.

Webrings: Websites linked to each other, all dealing with a similar subject and often listed on an index page.

WinZip: A useful piece of software for zipping and unzipping collections of files on computers with the Windows operating system. Files are zipped together to make them easier to move around the Internet.

WIPO: World Intellectual Property Organization. International body that aims to protect authors' and artists' rights worldwide.

Worm: A nasty virus program that can reproduce itself over a computer network. It usually attaches itself to another program and then proceeds to cause malicious damage to the user's computer such as shutting it down.

WYSIWYG: Stands for 'What You See Is What You Get' and describes the most popular way of working with a web page editor. With WYSIWYG designers place images and type text straight onto the page rather than having to insert HTML code. The HTML code is automatically generated by the editing program.

XML: Extensible Markup Language. Web pages created using data in a text file with context. It allows web designers to change the formatting of the page easily and create versions for interactive television, mobile phones and PDAs.

Zip: Refers to compressing files (making them take up less memory) so making them quicker to send over the Internet. There are various software tools available for 'zipping' and 'unzipping' files including PKZip and Winzip (for PC); Stuffit and ZipIt (for Mac). Zipped files usually have the file extension .zip.

Zip disk: A sophisticated floppy disk with up to 250Mb storage. This has a much greater capacity than an ordinary floppy disk and looks slightly larger and bulkier. Like floppies they are also re-recordable. Users need a Zip drive to be able to use a Zip disk.

Suggested reading

There are many great photography, computer and Internet books and magazines, but these ones were collected as this book was produced:

Web Design Index compiled by Günter Beer, published by The Pepin Press/Agile Rabbit Editions, ISBN 90-5768-063-7. (Recommended!)

The Photographer's Website Manual by Philip Andrews, published by RotoVision, ISBN 2-88046-713-6.

The Photographer's Internet Handbook by Joe Farace, published by Allworth Press, ISBN 1-58115-084-9.

HTML in Plain English by Sandra E Eddy, published by MIS: Press, ISBN 1-55828-587-3.

Digital Photo magazine, published in the United Kingdom by Emap Active.

ePHOTOzine website, published online by Magezine Publishing. Spelling of company name by Peter Bargh – can you see what he did there? Clever.

Photography Monthly magazine, published in the United Kingdom by Archant Group.

Practical Photography magazine, published in the United Kingdom by Emap Active.

Acknowledgments

This is the bit that's like a bad Oscars speech, but it's SO important. Thanks to:

Steven Booth at Transmission Media for the inspiration and the website, but hey, he got paid, didn't he?

Easily.co.uk for domain name help and virtual hosting. Adobe, Microsoft, Macromedia, Jasc/Corel, Nvu, IrfanView, Netscape and Ipswitch for software, some of which we actually paid for. BT Yahoo! and Tripod/Lycos for free test webspace.

Her Majesty's Stationery Office for the copyright act. *Practical Photography*, *Digital Photo*, *Photography Monthly*, *Internet*, *ePHOTOzine*, Emap Consumer Media and Dan Lezano for, er, something, I'm sure. BBC Webwise, *Encarta*

by Bloomsbury/Microsoft and FOLDOC – the Free On-Line Dictionary Of Computing for help compiling the glossary. The Internet Advertising Bureau for banner sizes.

Apple Computers for being… so different. Compaq's Presario for being… so normal. Nikon UK and Fujifilm UK for the loan of two excellent digital cameras, the Nikon D70 and the FinePix S3 Pro respectively.

Photographers Niall Clutton, Jesse Goff, Johnny Greig, Tim James, Carl De Keyzer, Bob Laughton, Martin Parr, Jo Pitson, Renegade Photo, Tim Sandall, Peter Stiles, Ashley G Watts and all the others who generously gave permission for their sites to appear – those that we couldn't fit in can be seen via www.websitesforphotographers.co.uk.

Lynda Elliott at InWeb Design for late-night email conversations about stuff we couldn't squeeze in. King Du Chinese restaurant – if their king prawn chow mein is as good as their website, it's worth a trip to Harlow. Nicola Hodgson and Ame Verso for bravely and brilliantly editing the one who considers himself 'The Editor'. And, of course, Laura, Charlotte and Katy who put up with a grumpy daddy dominating the computer for eight months.

About the author

Martyn Moore is a photographer and journalist. He has held a number of magazine editorships in the fields of photography, Internet technology and motoring, including Managing Editor and Editor-in-Chief of Emap photography magazines and editor of *Internet Magazine*, Britain's most popular web magazine. He is currently the editor of *Classic Cars* magazine; a contributor to the *Daily Telegraph* on motoring subjects and vehicles expert on BBC1's *20th Century Roadshow*.

PHOTO: KAREN ELLIOTT

Index